General editor: Graham Handley MA PhD

Brodie's Notes on William Shakespeare's

Hamlet

Sheila Mathieson MA
English Lecturer, Extra-Mural Department, London University

Pan Books London, Sydney and Auckland

First published 1985 by Pan Books Ltd
Cavaye Place, London SW10 9PG
19
© Pan Books Ltd, 1985
ISBN 0 330 50192 5
Photoset by Parker Typesetting Service, Leicester
Printed and bound in Great Britain by
Richard Clay Ltd, Bungay, Suffolk

Contents

References in these Notes are to the
Arden Shakespeare: *Hamlet*,
but the Notes may be used with
any edition of the play.

Preface

This student revision aid is based on the principle that in any close examination of Shakespeare's plays 'the text's the thing'. Seeing a performance, or listening to a tape or record of a performance, is essential and is in itself a valuable and stimulating experience in understanding and appreciation. However, a real evaluation of Shakespeare's greatness, of his universality and of the nature of his literary and dramatic art, can only be achieved by constant application to the texts of the plays themselves. These revised editions of Brodie's Notes are intended to supplement that process through detailed critical commentary.

The first aim of each book is to fix the whole play in the reader's mind by providing a concise summary of the plot, relating it back, where appropriate, to its source or sources. Subsequently the book provides a summary of each scene, followed by *critical comments*. These may convey its importance in the dramatic structure of the play, creation of atmosphere, indication of character development, significance of figurative language etc, and they will also explain or paraphrase difficult words or phrases and identify meaningful references. At the end of each act revision questions in ascending order of difficulty are set to test the student's specific and broad understanding and appreciation of the play.

An extended critical commentary follows this scene by scene analysis. This embraces such major elements as characterization, imagery, the use of blank verse and prose, soliloquies and other aspects of the play which the editor considers need close attention. The paramount aim is to send the reader back to the text. The book concludes with a series of revision questions which require a detailed knowledge of the play; the first of these has notes by the editor of what *might* be included in a written answer. The intention is to stimulate and to guide; the whole emphasis of this commentary is to encourage the student's *involvement* in the play, to develop disciplined critical responses and thus promote personal enrichment through the imaginative experience of our greatest writer.

Graham Handley

Shakespeare and the Elizabethan playhouse

William Shakespeare was born in Stratford-upon-Avon in 1564, and there are reasons to suppose that he came from a relatively prosperous family. He was probably educated at Stratford Grammar School and, at the age of eighteen, married Anne Hathaway, who was twenty-six. They had three children, a girl born shortly after their marriage, followed by twins in 1585 (the boy died in 1596). It seems likely that Shakespeare left for London shortly after a company of visiting players had visited Stratford in 1585, for by 1592 – according to the jealous testimony of one of his fellow-writers Robert Greene – he was certainly making his way both as actor and dramatist. The theatres were closed because of the plague in 1593; when they reopened Shakespeare worked with the Lord Chamberlain's men, later the King's men, and became a shareholder in each of the two theatres with which he was most closely associated, the Globe and the Blackfriars. He later purchased New Place, a considerable property in his home town of Stratford, to which he retired in 1611; there he entertained his great contemporary Ben Jonson (1572–1637) and the poet Michael Drayton (1563–1631). An astute businessman, Shakespeare lived comfortably in the town until his death in 1616.

This is a very brief outline of the life of our greatest writer, for little more can be said of him with certainty, though the plays – and poems – are living witness to the wisdom, humanity and many-faceted nature of the man. He was both popular and successful as a dramatist, perhaps less so as an actor. He probably began work as a dramatist in the late 1580s, by collaborating with other playwrights and adapting old plays, and by 1598 Francis Meres was paying tribute to his excellence in both comedy and tragedy. His first original play was probably *Love's Labour's Lost* (1590) and while the theatres were closed during the plague he wrote his narrative poems *Venus and Adonis* (1593) and *The Rape of Lucrece* (1594). The sonnets were almost certainly written in the 1590s, though not published until 1609; the first 126 are addressed to a young man who was his friend and patron, while the rest are concerned with the 'dark lady'.

The dating of Shakespeare's plays has exercised scholars ever since the publication of the First Folio (1623), listed them as comedies, histories and tragedies. It seems more important to look at them chronologically as far as possible, in order to trace Shakespeare's considerable development as a dramatist. The first period, say to the middle of the 1590s, included such plays as *Love's Labour's Lost*, *The Comedy of Errors*, *Richard III*, *The Taming of the Shrew*, *Romeo and Juliet* and *Richard II*. These early plays embrace the categories listed in the First Folio, so that Shakespeare the craftsman is evident in his capacity for variety of subject and treatment. The next phase includes *A Midsummer's Night's Dream*, *The Merchant of Venice*, *Henry IV Parts 1 and 2*, *Henry V* and *Much Ado About Nothing*, as well as *Julius Caesar*, *As You Like It* and *Twelfth Night*. These are followed, in the early years of the century, by his great tragic period: *Hamlet*, *Othello*, *King Lear* and *Macbeth*, with *Antony and Cleopatra* and *Coriolanus* belonging to 1607–09. The final phase embraces the romances (1610–13), *Cymbeline*, *The Tempest* and *The Winter's Tale* and the historical play *Henry VIII*.

Each of these revision aids will place the individual text under examination in the chronology of the remarkable dramatic output that spanned twenty years from the early 1590s to about 1613. The practical theatre for which Shakespeare wrote and acted derived from the inn courtyards in which performances had taken place, the few playhouses in his day being modelled on their structure. They were circular or hexagonal in shape, allowing the balconies and boxes around the walls full view of the stage. This large stage, which had no scenery, jutted out into the pit, the most extensive part of the theatre, where the poorer people – the 'groundlings' – stood. There was no roof (though the Blackfriars, used from 1608 onwards, was an indoor theatre) and thus bad weather meant no performance. Certain plays were acted at court, and these private performances normally marked some special occasion. Costumes, often rich ones, were used, and music was a common feature, with musicians on or under the stage; this sometimes had additional features, for example a trapdoor to facilitate the entry of a ghost. Women were barred by law from appearing on stage, and all female parts were played by boy actors; this undoubtedly explains the

many instances in Shakespeare where a woman has to conceal her identity by disguising herself as a man, e.g. Rosalind in *As You Like It*, Viola in *Twelfth Night*.

Shakespeare and his contemporaries often adapted their plays from sources in history and literature, extending an incident or a myth or creating a dramatic narrative from known facts. They were always aware of their own audiences, and frequently included topical references, sometimes of a satirical flavour, which would appeal to – and be understood by – the groundlings as well as their wealthier patrons who occupied the boxes. Shakespeare obviously learned much from his fellow dramatists and actors, being on good terms with many of them. Ben Jonson paid generous tribute to him in the lines prefaced to the First Folio of Shakespeare's plays:

Thou art a monument without a tomb,
And art alive still, while thy book doth live
And we have wits to read, and praise to give.

Among his contemporaries were Thomas Kyd (1558–94) and Christopher Marlowe (1564–93). Kyd wrote *The Spanish Tragedy*, the revenge motif here foreshadowing the much more sophisticated treatment evident in *Hamlet*, while Marlowe evolved the 'mighty line' of blank verse, a combination of natural speech and elevated poetry. The quality and variety of Shakespeare's blank verse owes something to the innovatory brilliance of Marlowe but it is imbued with the stamp of individuality, richness of associations, technical virtuosity and, above all, the genius of imaginative power.

The texts of Shakespeare's plays are still mines for scholars, and the editors of these revision aids have used the Arden editions of Shakespeare, which are regarded as pre-eminent for their scholarly approach. They are strongly recommended for advanced students, but other editions, like The New Penguin Shakespeare, The New Swan, The Signet are all good annotated editions currently available. A reading list of selected reliable works on the play being studied is provided at the end of each commentary and students are advised to turn to these as their interest in the play deepens.

Literary terms used in these notes

Alliteration Repetition of a consonant through several words, e.g. 'And I do doubt the hatch and the disclose/Will be some danger.'

Antithesis Contrasting words which express contrasting ideas, e.g. 'My words fly up, my thoughts remain below'.

Irony Expressing meaning by saying the opposite; it is often done unconsciously, e.g. 'And the King's rouse the heaven shall bruit again/Re-speaking earthly thunder' (Claudius is unknowingly fore-telling his own doom).

Dramatic irony The effectiveness of a scene depends partly upon a character's words and actions being the opposite of what is in fact happening, e.g. in Act III, Scene 1 Claudius agrees 'with all my heart,/It doth much content me' to watch the Players' performance without realizing that it has been set up to expose his guilt.

Image One object or idea used to express another, e.g. 'Virtue itself scapes not calumnious strokes./The canker galls the infants of the spring'.

Metaphor Expressing one thing directly in terms of another, without using 'as' or 'like', e.g. 'How weary, stale, flat and unprofitable/Seem to me all the uses of this world!/Fie on't, ah fie, 'tis an unweeded garden.'

Personification Addressing an object as if it were a person, e.g. 'But look, the morn in russet mantle clad/Walks o'er the dew of yon high eastward hill.'

Pun Playing with two or more meanings of a single word, e.g. in Act I, Scene 2 'son' used by Claudius, picked up as 'sun' by Hamlet.

Simile Explaining one thing in terms of another using the words 'as' or 'like', e.g. 'Now see that noble and most sovereign reason/Like sweet bells jangled out of tune and harsh.'

Symbol Using one thing to stand for another or for a series of things, e.g. the Ghost, 'Be thou a spirit of health/Or goblin damned.'

The play
Plot

Hamlet, son of the late King of Denmark, is in a mood of world-weariness. His mother has married her brother-in-law Claudius and he now reigns. Within two months of his father's death Hamlet is visited by his father's ghost, who informs him that he was murdered by Claudius. Upon Hamlet falls the duty of revenge, but he feels himself ill-suited for it: 'The time is out of joint: O cursed spite/That ever I was born to set it right.' Consequently he is glad of excuses to put it off. Hamlet decides to feign madness so that people will not pay much attention to what he is seriously plotting, and because he has been really unsettled by the shock of the news; if he betrays the fact little notice will be taken if he is supposed to be mad. Polonius, a councillor of State, is quite certain that the reason for Hamlet's madness is that he has forbidden his daughter Ophelia to return Hamlet's affection. Claudius is not convinced that this is the reason.

The visit of a troupe of players affords Hamlet the opportunity of discovering whether the message from the ghost is authentic; he arranges for a play to be acted at Court reproducing the circumstances of his father's murder and watches the King's reactions to it. The result leaves him in no doubt that the King is guilty. But Claudius now realizes his crime is found out and quickly makes counterplans to send Hamlet away on a diplomatic mission to England. Meanwhile Hamlet has an interview with his mother, strongly rebukes her for her hasty remarriage, and tries to make her promise not to live with Claudius as a wife. During the interview an eavesdropper gives himself away. Hamlet makes a thrust with his rapier in the direction of the sound and the eavesdropper falls dead. It is Polonius.

The King now fears for himself: 'It had been so with us had we been there'; the murder in the palace of such an important person puts him in an awkward position, so Claudius decides to send Hamlet to England immediately with Rosencrantz and Guildenstern. They carry a secret commission exhorting the

King of England to put Hamlet to instant death. Claudius tells Hamlet that the reason for his sudden departure is his safety since, as the murderer of Polonius, he is in danger. But Hamlet is suspicious, steals the commission when he is on board ship, finds the command for his own death, and replaces it with a commission exhorting the instant deaths of the two bearers. Shortly afterwards, in a fight with pirates, Hamlet is taken prisoner. In consideration of a good turn he is able to do them however, the pirates land him in Denmark.

Hamlet returns just in time to witness Ophelia's funeral. Grief for her father's death has driven her mad, and she has drowned herself. At the funeral Hamlet grapples with Laertes, son of Polonius, recalled home from Paris by the news of his father's death. Laertes rages against Hamlet as the murderer of his father and indirectly of his sister. The King's first plan for the murder of Hamlet having failed, he arranges another with Laertes. Laertes is to challenge Hamlet to a duel with foils, but Laertes is to have an unblunted rapier. Laertes adds the suggestion that the rapier be poisoned. In case this plan should fail, as a second line of attack the King proposes the preparation of a goblet of poisoned wine which Hamlet should be encouraged to drink when he is hot and thirsty. The first part of the plan works as arranged and Laertes wounds Hamlet; but in a scuffle the duellists change rapiers and Hamlet wounds Laertes with his own unblunted, poisoned weapon. It is the Queen who drinks the poisoned wine.

At the point of death Laertes reveals the King's treachery. In a fit of rage Hamlet does what he has been unable to do in cold blood: he stabs Claudius with the poisoned rapier he is still holding. In a few seconds the King is dead.

Dying from his own poisoned wound, Hamlet begs his close friend Horatio to give a true report of him and his cause to the world. The play ends with the entrance of Fortinbras whom Hamlet has named as the successor to the throne.

Source

The immediate source for Shakespeare's play was an earlier play on the same subject, usually called the *Ur-Hamlet*. Although never printed, this play is known to have been performed on several occasions during the late 1580s and 1590s, and may have been written by Thomas Kyd. Little is known about the *Ur-Hamlet*, other than that it was a revenge tragedy which contained a ghost and a revenger named Hamlet whose origins were Danish.

The Hamlet story can be traced back to the *Historiae Danicae*, published in 1514, but written at the end of the twelfth century by Saxo. His writings include stories of the murder of a brother, an incestuous marriage, pretended madness, and revenge. There are also some remarkable similarities with Shakespeare's play in the dialogue, for instance that between Hamlet and his mother; furthermore the characters of Ophelia, Rosencrantz, Guildenstern and Polonius are foreshadowed in Saxo's work.

Saxo's writings were retold in French by Belleforest in his *Histoires Tragiques*, published between 1559 and 1582. Belleforest elaborated some aspects of the stories: for example, in his account the ghost asks his son for vengeance.

Shakespeare would certainly have been familiar with the *Ur-Hamlet*. He may have known Belleforest's work. He was certainly familiar with other revenge plays like Kyd's *The Spanish Tragedy*, which were popular in the late 1580s – plays in which revenge was accompanied by many deaths, bloodthirsty violence, and frequently acts of incest, and where the central character was of the melancholy type. In writing *Hamlet* Shakespeare, a true man of the theatre, was following a tradition that was popular at the time.

Date

Hamlet was almost certainly written in 1601. It was entered on the Stationers' Register in July 1602. It was not mentioned by Francis Meres in a list of plays he recorded in 1598. The mention within the play of the 'little eyases' is almost certainly a reference to the boy actors who played at Blackfriars after 1600; thus it is most unlikely that the play existed before that date.

Scene summaries, critical comment, textual notes and revision questions

Act I Scene 1

Barnardo relieves Francisco at midnight as sentinel on the battlements of Elsinore castle. Horatio and Marcellus arrive to watch with Barnardo for the appearance of the Ghost of Hamlet, former King of Denmark. While they are talking about the Ghost he appears and walks silently across the stage, although challenged to speak. After his departure Horatio expresses his fear that some disaster is about to befall the state. The discussion moves on to the preparations for war against Norway, and conditions within Denmark are compared to the situation in Rome after the murder of Julius Caesar. The Ghost reappears and Marcellus attempts unsuccessfully to strike him with his pike. At that moment day breaks and the Ghost disappears. Horatio resolves to tell young Hamlet, his friend and the dead King's son, of what has happened.

Commentary

This first scene in the play sets a mood of fear, foreboding and unrest, which is created in the opening lines by the alertness of the Sentinels and the tense, staccato form of their questions. The darkness, the cold, the quiet, and Francisco's words 'I am sick at heart', reinforce the atmosphere.

The dramatic suspense is continued with Francisco's challenge to Horatio, and is heightened by the two appearances of the Ghost, whose total silence adds to the fear of the watchers.

The Ghost, an indication of a dead spirit unable to rest, may portend disaster; the possible magnitude of this disaster is shown in Horatio's speech recalling the death of Julius Caesar, and in the crowing of the cock, which gains greater import by being spread through the four basic elements of earth, air, water and fire.

The atmosphere of fear and the dramatic suspense is lowered at the end of the scene with the coming of the dawn, expressed in vivid and beautiful metaphor.

Another function of this opening scene is to provide factual information: the war between Denmark and Norway, in which Fortinbras of Norway was defeated; the death of Hamlet, King of Denmark; new preparations for war between Denmark and Norway. This threat of war increases the sense of unrest in the scene and introduces the theme of violence, which is demonstrated visually in Marcellus's attempt to strike the Ghost.

It is a scene of action: in the movements of the Sentinels; in the many entries and exits of the characters; in the stalking of the Ghost; and in the vivid descriptions of the preparations for war; and it forms a contrast to the more introspective scenes that are to follow.

The sense of dread is reinforced by the repetition of words suggesting a range of fear, and by the supernatural overtones of the scene's imagery. Conflict is reinforced by antithesis, of night and day, of life and death.

At the end of the scene the mood of fear is reduced by the imagery of the bird of dawning which dispels the terrors of the night, and by the reference to 'our Saviour's birth'; this gives a hint of hope with the introduction of the young Hamlet.

unfold Reveal.
carefully ... hour Punctually.
rivals Companions.
ground Country.
Give you May God grant you.
approve our eyes Confirm.
scholar Latin was supposed to have a greater power in exorcising spirits.
together with Assuming the shape of.
buried Denmark The dead King of Denmark.
sensible Made aware through the senses.
avouch Evidence.
Norway King of Norway.
parle Conference.
sledded Polacks Polish soldiers in sledges.
jump Precisely.
in the gross ... opinion In my general view.
strange eruption Abnormal violent occurrence.
nightly toils the subject Makes the people work at night.
brazen Bronze.
mart Trade.
impress Compulsory service to the state.

sore Wearying.
does not divide. . . week Allows no rest day on Sunday.
toward Imminent.
prick'd on Urged on.
emulate Jealous.
stood seiz'd of Owned.
a moiety competent A suitable area of land.
gaged Offered as a pledge.
carriage . . . design'd Details of the prepared agreement.
unimproved mettle Untested spirit.
skirts Outlying parts.
for food and diet For payment of their keep.
hath a stomach in't Needs courage (the 'eating' metaphor is extended through these lines).
terms compulsatory Imposed terms.
source of Cause of (the metaphor is continued in 'head', fountainhead).
rummage Great activity.
sort Suit.
portentous Foreshadowing significant events.
mote A disturbing occurrence.
palmy Thriving (the palm signifies victory).
stars . . . fire Comets (believed to warn of disaster).
Disasters in the sun Ominous signs (caused by unfavourable dispositions of the planets).
moist star Moon.
still Always.
climatures Country (with the same climate).
cross it Confront it.
happily Maybe.
partisan A long-handled spear used by infantry.
hies Hurries.
confine The place to which he belongs.
made probation Made plain.
'gainst A little before.
strike Threaten disaster.
takes Threatens evil.

Act I Scene 2

King Claudius regrets his brother Hamlet's death, but rejoices in his marriage to Hamlet's widow, Gertrude. He dismisses the threat to Denmark from young Fortinbras of Norway, and dispatches two ambassadors, Cornelius and Voltemand, with messages of greeting to the old King of Norway. Claudius turns his attention to the request of Laertes, son of the Lord Chamberlain, to be allowed to return to his studies in Paris; having obtained agreement from Laertes's father Polonius, Claudius gives him permission to leave. He turns next to young Hamlet, and with the Queen urges him to put aside his mourning for his father's death, reminding him that everyone must die. Supported by the Queen he asks Hamlet not to return to his studies in Wittenberg, but to remain at Court in Denmark. In a soliloquy Hamlet expresses his longing for death and his despair and disgust at his mother's hasty remarriage. Horatio enters with Marcellus and Barnardo and tells Hamlet of the appearance of his father's Ghost. Hamlet resolves to watch for him with them that night.

Commentary

This scene offers a contrast to the previous one. It is set at Court, with the formality and splendour which that involves, and the stage is full of people. Hamlet's black clothes stand out against the dress of the other figures. The scene introduces most of the other characters in the play.

The King's first speech is elegant and controlled, and although he opens with his sorrow at the death of old Hamlet, the ease with which he passes on to his pleasure in marriage suggests that his sorrow is little more than superficial. The careful way he balances sorrow and joy seems almost too structured to be an expression of deep feeling, and his repetition of 'dear brother's death' adds to this impression of a lack of spontaneity. There is a sense of something being hidden. His concern with Norway suggests an interest in matters of state, but it is with great ease that he delegates these matters to other people, again implying that his interest is superficial.

Laertes forms a dramatic contrast in the play to Hamlet, and the freedom that is granted him to continue his studies abroad is set beside the constraints put upon Hamlet by Claudius later in the scene to remain in the Court.

Polonius is presented first here in the play in his most significant role, that of a father; the verbose quality of his language is marked, even in such a short speech.

In his speeches with Hamlet Claudius is clearly trying to overcome Hamlet's opposition to him. The language at this point becomes much more poetic, with the development of the image of the garden, of the sun (with the punning on son), of food and eating, and the introduction of words such as 'nature' and 'black' which recur with many associations throughout the play. There is a sense of genuine feeling in Claudius here. Hamlet's skill with language reflects the many layers of his personality and the complexity of his introspection. In contrast, the simplicity of the Queen's language echoes her ready acceptance of her marriage with Claudius and the ease with which she put the death of her former husband behind her.

Claudius's reasoned speech to Hamlet has the qualities of a father's advice to a son; like his earlier speeches it seems too carefully crafted to be the result of spontaneous feeling; his concern is above all for himself. His lack of perception of Hamlet's true feelings is underlined when he returns to his revelry. The action of the play is to give an intense significance to his words 'And the King's rouse the heaven shall bruit again', but Claudius is unaware of the irony.

Hamlet's soliloquy reveals the depth of his despair at his mother's hasty remarriage. The classical references create a formality which intensifies Hamlet's conception of her behaviour as unnatural. The speech is fragmented, with broken lines, questions, exclamations, parentheses, which echo his despair and contrast strongly with Claudius's carefully prepared speeches. The impression is of an out-pouring of feeling, leaving nothing hidden. The end of his speech shows his fear of the outcome of his mother's remarriage, a fear which is justified by the action of the second part of the scene.

Hamlet's joy in seeing Horatio is a genuine expression of feeling, and is immediately contrasted with the bitterness of his feelings over the marriage. The atmosphere becomes tense when Horatio asks where Hamlet saw his father, revealing Horatio's sensitivity and fear concerning the Ghost, and the scene is raised to a higher pitch of tension through his vivid, detailed account of the Ghost's appearance. The contrast between the slow pace of most lines and the repeated 'p' sounds of the lines describing the Ghost's appearance, creates an atmosphere of fear and excitement. The quick interchange of question and answer which follows intensifies this, culminating in Hamlet's determination to speak with the Ghost, a determination which reveals his courage. The final couplet of the scene makes a general statement of universal belief, which leads forward into the ensuing action.

contracted ... woe Joined in sorrow.
dropping Weeping. (This line introduces a series of antitheses which reflect the conflict Hamlet feels.)
weak supposal Poor opinion.
out of frame Disordered.
gait herein Going forward in this matter.
full proportions Necessary numbers.
dilated Described at length.
slow leave Reluctant permission.
A little more ... kind Close in relationship, but lacking the natural feelings of a son.
sun Pun on 'son'; the image is developed through the word 'nighted' and the following 'black' associations.
nighted clothes Mourning clothes; also, depressed mood.
particular ... thee To affect you so strongly.
windy suspiration ... breath Deep sighing.
dejected haviour Downcast look.
as any ... sense As anything which is familiar to our senses.
corse Corpse.
cousin Commonly used for 'relation'.
rouse Drinking session.
bruit Noise abroad.
sullied Suggests both 'solid' and 'contaminated'.
resolve Dissolve.
unweeded garden A repeated image in the play.
merely Entirely.
Hyperion The Sun God in classical mythology.
satyr Part man, part goat.
beteem Allow.
Niobe The personification of maternal sorrow. According to Greek legend she wept for her children slain by Apollo. Her grief turned her to stone from which tears would periodically trickle down the rock face.
galled Made sore.
dexterity Speed.
incestuous Marriage with a husband's brother was considered incest.
admiration Amazement.
attent Attentive.
upon the witness Witnessed by
at point exactly Correctly.
cap-à-pie From top to toe.

Appears before Note that the change to the present tense increases the immediacy and impact of Horatio's account.

oppress'd Taken by surprise.

truncheon A staff denoting military office.

distill'd Transformed.

beaver Faceguard of a helmet.

grizzled Grey.

a sable silver'd Black with some silver hairs.

though hell ... gape Hamlet's determination is in contrast to the inadequacy he expressed earlier.

requite Repay.

doubt Suspect. The appearance of a ghost would foretell evil to an Elizabethan audience.

o'erwhelm Cover over.

Act I Scene 3

Laertes warns Ophelia not to take Hamlet's attentions too seriously. Before he leaves for Paris, Polonius advises his son about his behaviour, then reinforces his warnings to Ophelia, suggesting that Hamlet is only trifling with her; Polonius orders her to spend no more time with Hamlet. Ophelia agrees to his request.

Commentary

This scene is more intimate than Scene 2, allowing deeper insight into the three characters present. Laertes's speech creates a mood of natural conversation with lines that run on fluently. His language is poetic, enhanced by imagery of the moon, and of treasure; the effect of the loss of virginity is expressed powerfully in disease imagery, which links ironically with the garden imagery of the previous scene.

Ophelia says little, but shows spirit and common sense in asking Laertes not to give her advice which he would not himself follow.

Polonius's entry delays Laertes's departure further. His advice to Laertes is a series of commands, reflecting his organizing personality. In his conversation with Ophelia his language becomes increasingly repetitive, complex and unstructured, suggesting his growing anxiety at her situation. He allows her to say very little, and scorns her words.

convoy is assistant Means of transport is available.
Hold Consider.
toy in blood Passing fancy. 'Toy': whim, trifle; 'blood': passion.
primy In its prime.
suppliance Fulfilling of need.
in thews and bulk In strength and size.
temple Soul and body.
cautel Craftiness.
greatness weighed High birth considered.
state This reflects the Elizabethan idea that there must be moral health in the ruling family for the state to flourish; the idea is expressed by Hamlet and others in the play.
body The metaphor of the state as a body, with head, limbs etc., is frequent in Shakespeare, and is connected with the health theme noted above.
credent Trusting.
list Hear.
chaste treasure open Lose your virginity.
chariest Most cautious.
scapes Escapes.
calumnious Slanderous.
canker ... buttons The worm destroys the buds (of the rose).
blastments Shrivellings.
ungracious i.e. lacking spiritual sincerity.
recks ... rede Does not follow his own advice.
precepts Rules.
character Write.
unproportion'd Wild.
adoption Friendship.
Grapple Fasten with grappling irons.
courage One who is first with new fashion.
Take ... censure Listen to ... views.
husbandry Economy.
tend Wait.
tenders Expressions.
green Ignorant.
Unsifted Inexperienced.
tender me a fool Pun: 'make a fool of me' and 'offer me a fool', i.e. Ophelia.
importun'd Pressed.
springes to catch woodcocks i.e. snares, traps for birds.
blood burns Sexual desire is aroused – the fire image is developed in the following lines.
prodigal Recklessly.
entreatments Discussion.
larger tether More freedom.

brokers Dealers in things of value – these lines play on monetary dealings and sexual dealings, and belittle Hamlet's feelings for Ophelia.

Act I Scene 4

Hamlet, Horatio and Marcellus watch for the Ghost on the castle battlements. Hearing the sound of trumpets which accompany the King's drinking, Hamlet regrets the reputation for revelry which Denmark is acquiring abroad, and considers how far one weakness can corrupt a human being. The Ghost appears, and beckons a horrified Hamlet to follow him. His companions urge him to remain with them, indicating the possible dangers of going with the Ghost, but Hamlet is determined to go. Horatio and Marcellus follow some distance behind Hamlet, expressing their concern at the possible significance of the Ghost.

Commentary

This scene returns us to the castle battlements; the short lines, the reference to the cold, the rhythm of the words 'nipping' and 'eager', the question about the time and the reference to the midnight hour, all convey the tension and suspense of waiting. The distant sounds of trumpet and drum remind everyone that the King is at his revels, ignorant of the threat imposed by the Ghost. Hamlet's criticism of the King's drinking session contrasts with his own concern at Denmark's reputation for revelry under the new King. The language underlines this contrast with the long vowel sounds and alliterated 'd's of 'drains his draughts of Rhenish down' and the short vowels of 'kettle-drum and trumpet' with the alliterated 't's.

Hamlet's long speech moves to general considerations of human nature through 'some vicious mole of nature'; the threatening mood of the scene is maintained by the image of the mole with its dark colour and associations of being under the ground, and by the imagery of war (pales and forts). The complexity and length of this speech emphasize Hamlet's awareness of the possible import of the event he is about to witness; this is shown also in his reference to 'Nature's livery or Fortune's star.'

Hamlet's horror at the appearance of the Ghost, shown in his

appeal to 'Angels and ministers of grace', builds up the atmosphere of fear in the scene. He addresses the Ghost in a manner
that is dignified and respectful, appropriate to the picture which
has already been given of the dead King. The many words in
this speech associated with death add to the horror of the
occasion and anticipate the events which are to come, as does the
ponderous style of the speech. The quick interchange that follows increases the tension again; Hamlet's courage and determination stand out in contrast to the fear expressed by Horatio and
Marcellus.

Horatio's speech, with its imagery of sea cliffs and repetition
of words associated with horror and dread, echoes Hamlet's fear
that the Ghost may be a manifestation of the devil. His extended
sea metaphor suggests the magnitude of the event they are
witnessing. His discussion of madness is ironic, unconsciously
anticipating the madness that apparently affects Hamlet later in
the play.

Hamlet's mention of the 'Nemean lion' also underlines the
magnitude of what he is about to do. His language is vigorous,
showing the energy with which he follows the Ghost. Tension
and fear are increased again at the end by the single line
speeches of Horatio and Marcellus, and their recognition of the
significance of the Ghost's appearance, relating it to the 'rotten'
state of Denmark.

shrewdly Bitterly.
eager Biting.
wake Celebrate.
traduc'd Exposed to contempt.
tax'd Condemned by.
clepe Call.
the pith . . . attribute The essential quality of our success.
mole Defect.
guilty Responsible.
complexion A reference to the predominance of one of the four
  humours, blood, choler, melancholy, phlegm, from which man's body
  was believed to be made up.
pales Fences.
plausive Praiseworthy.
dout Extinguish.
canoniz'd Consecrated.
cerements Grave clothes.

in complete steel In full armour.
horridly Causing horror.
disposition Mind.
beetles o'er Overhangs.
toys Impulsive ideas.
artire Vein.
Nemean lion Hercules's first labour was to slay the Nemean lion.
lets Stands in my way.
Have after Let's go after him.

Act I Scene 5

Hamlet and the Ghost converse alone; the Ghost tells Hamlet
that he was murdered by Claudius. Horatio and Marcellus enter
and, prompted by the voice of the Ghost from below the stage,
swear never to repeat what they have witnessed. Hamlet tells
them that he intends to feign madness. In a final soliloquy he
expresses his despair at the task he has to perform, that of
revenging his father's death.

Commentary

The atmosphere of fear is increased with the entry of the Ghost
and Hamlet, by the fragmented lines of the opening dialogue,
and the imagery of hell. Hamlet shows determination and sympathy, though these turn to shock at the Ghost's mention of
'revenge', shown in the brevity of his question 'What?'. The
Ghost's speech intensifies the horror, through the many words
associated with hell fire, and the 'stars' and 'porcupine' similes,
and through the contrasts of 'freeze thy young blood'. The
tension is maintained as the Ghost's account is broken up by
another fragmented dialogue, indicating Hamlet's shocked
sense of horror in his brief responses, and by the repetition of
'murder' and 'revenge'. The Ghost arouses Hamlet's involvement and emotion, and that of the audience, by his lyrical
evocation of the love he had for Gertrude, phrased in language
which is rhythmical and simple. The mention of the coming
dawn creates tension again, and the Ghost's speech has a sense
of urgency as it moves in narrative form through an account of
the murder. Drama and horror are created by the emphasis on
disease, and by the repeated contrasts in this speech between

death and disease, and life and health, brought to a climax in the image of polluted milk, the first nourishment after birth. The speech reaches another climax with the repetition of 'O horrible', and moves into a series of commands to Hamlet. The mood is changed briefly by the poetic reference to the coming dawn; the suggestion that 'fire' will be quelled, implies that the horror will be dispelled by Hamlet, and the darkness of horror will change into light.

Hamlet's speech plunges the audience back into horror, with its shocked questions, short phrases and repetitions, reaching a climax in the repeated emphasis 'villain'. The brief phrases of his interchange with Horatio and Marcellus emphasize the stress he is experiencing, and there is a hint of madness in his excited addresses to the Ghost. The voice from beneath the stage creates a sense of hell, the hell in which Hamlet now finds himself, the hell that Denmark has become; it also reminds Hamlet that the Ghost may be an incarnation of the devil.

The scene ends on a serious note, taking the audience on into the play, with Hamlet's plans to feign madness; his final words, in the form of a rhyming couplet, recall the extent of the disorder and, emphasized by alliteration and short vowels and consonants, reflect Hamlet's despair that it is he who must act to change things.

in my days of nature During my life.
start from their spheres The stellar metaphor indicates disorder.
combined Twined together.
porpentine Porcupine.
eternal blazon Description of life after death.
weed Recurring image in the play, suggesting the growth of things unhealthy to the state.
Lethe River of the Underworld in classical mythology.
forged process Invented description.
prophetic soul Intuition.
secure hour Hour of relaxation.
hebenon Substance with a poisonous juice.
leperous Causing scales to form.
gates and alleys The metaphor of the body as a city was common in Elizabethan literature.
posset Grow thick (warm milk added to wine or ale).
tetter bark'd about Skin disease spread over.
lazar-like Like leprosy.

Unhousel'd Without receiving the Eucharist.
unanel'd Without the Last Rites.
reck'ning Confession of sins.
nature Natural instincts.
couple hell Embark upon evil deeds.
globe Head, with a pun on the Globe Theatre.
table Record.
fond Foolish.
saws Sayings.
pressures Impressions.
Hillo, ho, ho The language used by a falconer calling to his hawk,
  taken up by Hamlet in the following line.
more circumstance Explanation of detail.
whirling Excited.
Saint Patrick The patron saint of Ireland.
honest ghost The ghost of his father, not a demon.
truepenny Honest man.
hic et ubique? Here and everywhere.
pioner Digger.
bear myself Behave.
antic disposition Strange behaviour, suggestive of madness.
encumber'd Crossed.
aught Anything.
out of joint Completely disordered.

Revision questions on Act I

1 Describe the opening scene of the play, drawing attention to its dramatic importance.
2 How does Shakespeare convey to the audience necessary information concerning events that have occurred before the play begins?
3 What is your impression of the character of Hamlet at the end of Act I?
4 Select two images which recur in Act I and show how they contribute to the dramatic events and revelations of this first act.

Act II Scene 1

Polonius instructs his servant Reynaldo to spy on Laertes in Paris, suggesting that he questions Laertes's friends and spreads false gossip in his efforts to discover the truth. Reynaldo is shocked at these suggestions, but agrees to do as Polonius commands and departs. Ophelia enters, terrified by a visit she has received from Hamlet, whose clothes were in disorder, and who behaved very strangely. Polonius, convinced that Hamlet's behaviour is the result of thwarted love, regrets that he has misjudged Hamlet's intentions; they leave to tell the King about this incident.

Commentary

In this scene Polonius's character is developed further, revealing his suspicious and devious nature. His language is verbose and fragmented, with many unconnected images, long sentences and many interjections, numerous adjectives qualifying everything he says. His lack of clarity is shown particularly when even he loses track of what he had been saying ('what was I about to say?'), and is emphasized by the change into prose at this moment in the scene. It is underlined further by Reynaldo's brief, straightforward statements.

Ophelia's account of Hamlet's behaviour is in contrast clear and vivid. The detail with which she describes 'a little shaking of mine arm ... and end his being' and the many 's' sounds which she uses suggest the depth of feeling she has experienced, and the depth of suffering which overwhelms Hamlet.

Danskers Danes.
keep Lodge.
encompassment . . . drift Roundabout and indirect form.
forgeries Lies.
rank Scandalous, a word often linked in the play with 'weeds' meaning 'foul'.
slips Lapses in behaviour.
drabbing Associating with whores.
season Modify.
incontinency Licentiousness.
quaintly Skilfully.
unreclaimed Wild.
of general assault Common to all men.
fetch of warrant Legitimate device.
sullies See note p.20 on 'sullied'.
converse Discussion.
prenominate Already mentioned.
be assur'd Make sure.

closes with ... consequence Agrees with you in the following manner.

the addition The way of address.

Videlicet Namely.

reach Thought.

windlasses The implication is by indirect means.

assays of bias Devious trials, an image from the game of bowls (Polonius jumps from image to image in this speech).

have me Understand me.

observe ... yourself Go along with whatever he wishes.

unbrac'd Undone.

foul'd Dirty.

down-gyved Hanging round his ankles.

in purport In appearance.

loosed ... horrors Dramatic irony, for Hamlet has spoken with the Ghost, and the audience knows this.

Mad Irony again; Hamlet has spoken of assuming madness.

goes ... arm Goes backward until he touches her with his arm outstretched. The change to the present tense increases the drama of Ophelia's account.

ecstasy Madness.

property Nature.

fordoes Destroys.

quoted Watched.

wrack Ruin.

beshrew ... jealousy! A plague on my suspicion.

cast ... ourselves Be too suspicious ('cast' is an image from hunting).

being kept ... love Keeping it secret might cause more grief than revealing it will cause hatred.

Act II Scene 2

The King welcomes Rosencrantz and Guildenstern, whom he has invited to court to try to find out the cause of Hamlet's strange behaviour. Polonius announces the arrival of Norwegian ambassadors, and then on their departure, explains that Hamlet's madness is caused by his thwarted love for Ophelia. He suggests to the King that they should spy on a meeting between Hamlet and Ophelia. Hamlet meets Rosencrantz and Guildenstern, suspects the reason behind their visit to Denmark, and learns from them of the arrival of a favourite group of travelling players. He welcomes the players, and asks them to perform before the King 'The Murder of Gonzalo', into which he will insert some lines. In a final soliloquy Hamlet bemoans his inability to carry out his dead father's request, and describes how he will use the actors to expose Claudius's guilt.

Commentary

Claudius expresses his concern at Hamlet's strange behaviour and his desire to know the cause, in his opening speech. The irony of his final words, 'lies within our remedy', is powerfully dramatic, and suggests that Claudius's concern is more for himself than for Hamlet. In contrast the Queen is genuinely concerned for Hamlet, shown through the urgency of 'beseech' and 'instantly' and the long vowels of 'my too much changed son'.

Polonius shows his egoism and excitement in the fragmented nature of his first speech, and his desire to keep everyone in suspense while the ambassadors are admitted. Their announcement is important to the plot of the play; it establishes a reason for Fortinbras's presence in Denmark.

Polonius's convoluted and verbose style of speech is commented on by the Queen in her request for 'more matter with less art'; his inability to recognize her rebuke underlines again his self-centred nature. This is further reinforced by his frustrating and insensitive criticism of the style of Hamlet's flowery letter to Ophelia, and by the sense of an intrusion into her privacy. His egoism is clear in his demand to know the King's opinion of him, and his assurance that he 'will find where truth is hid'; the irony in this statement, for he is wrong in assuming that Ophelia's rejection is the sole cause of Hamlet's behaviour, emphasizes the falseness of his self-assurance, and the King's ambiguous answer, 'not that I know', adds to this. There is an additional ironic emphasis in the continuation of his words, 'though it were hid indeed within the centre'; the truth about Hamlet's despair lies with the King, at the centre of the state. Polonius's statement that he will 'loose' Ophelia to Hamlet introduces the sexual appetite theme which pervades the play and runs through Polonius's conversation with Hamlet, which is packed with puns. Hamlet's wit shows Polonius to be foolish and self-satisfied; he does not realize how Hamlet is scoring off him. Hamlet's apparently meaningless remarks establish meaning through successive puns.

The sexual theme is continued in Hamlet's conversation with

Rosencrantz and Guildenstern, in prose, through the metaphor of the body. The depth of his despair is clear in his speech of explanation; the rich imagery of the sky, balanced by his description of man, is submerged in disease imagery.

Hamlet's discussion with the Players, which includes references to contemporary Elizabethan events and theatre, shows no hint of madness. The mood changes again with the re-entry of Polonius. These swift changes of mood show the two sides of Hamlet; one witty, biting, apparently irrational, the other warm and interested in his friends. His joking with the young Player emphasizes the second side.

Hamlet's soliloquy at the end of the scene reveals the depth of his despair through a build-up of emotion in his portrayal of the Player and the following rhetorical questions. In contrasting the Player's assumed emotion and his own inaction, he vividly presents his self-disgust, which reaches a climax in the kite image, in the list of adjectives depicting his feelings for Claudius, and in the image of himself as a whore. The short lines of the speech draw further attention to his mood. The soliloquy ends on a calmer note, with more rhythmical language, as he makes his plans.

Sith Since.

exterior . . . inward The antithesis here underlines, as elsewhere in the play, the contrast between what is, and what seems to be; this is emphasized by 'resembles'.

neighbour'd Familiar with.

open'd Brought into the open. Irony; the King's behaviour is one cause of Hamlet's state of mind.

gentry Courtesy.

dread Held in great respect.

in the full bent Completely (metaphor from archery).

feast The metaphor is carried on by the King with a pun on 'grace'.

sift him Question him closely.

Upon our first Upon our first raising the subject.

falsely borne in hand Deceived.

arrests Orders to stop (the present tense makes the account more vivid).

assay See note p.29.

likes Pleases.

brevity Humorous irony; Polonius is rarely brief.

More . . . art Come to the point.

Perpend Consider.
ill at ... numbers Lack skill in writing these verses.
machine Body.
play'd ... table book Acted as go-between.
given my ... winking Closed my eyes to it.
out of thy star Outside your social sphere.
prescripts Advice.
lightness Lightheadedness.
by this declension Declining in this way.
arras Tapestry hung on the wall (named after Arras the town in France, famous for its tapestries).
board Greet.
fishmonger i.e. to fish out a secret; a reference to Polonius's enthusiasm for spying. Also 'procuror', another sexual reference.
good kissing carrion i.e. good for the sun to kiss. Sexual allusions abound in these lines.
conception Pregnancy; and understanding.
matter Subject matter; understood by Hamlet as 'dispute'.
purging Giving out.
amber Resin.
honesty Acceptable behaviour.
pregnant Meaningful. The sexual theme continues.
indifferent Ordinary, average.
we are not ... button We are not at the height of our good fortune (the body metaphor is developed in the following lines).
privates Ordinary men; (with pun on 'private parts').
bodies Substance.
wait upon Accompany.
beaten Familiar.
too dear a halfpenny Too dear at (or by) a halfpenny.
consonancy Harmonious friendship.
your discovery Your revealing (the reason for your coming).
o'erhanging firmament ... fire The sky; (also the canopy over the stage of the Elizabethan Globe Theatre).
fretted Decorated.
express Perfectly shaped.
quintessence Essential qualities.
Lenten Poor (like the limitations on pleasure imposed in Lent).
coted Overtook (a metaphor from coursing with dogs).
target Shield.
gratis In vain.
whose lungs ... sear Who laugh easily.
inhibition Difficulty.
wonted Accustomed.
eyrie Company; also the nest of a hawk or eagle.
eyases Young hawks (the fledgeling metaphor is developed here).

tyrannically Vigorously.

berattle Hold forth noisily.

goose-quills Pens (of writers of satire).

escotted Provided for.

quality Acting profession.

succession Future life.

tar Incite.

argument Discussion; also, the plot of a play.

appurtenance ... welcome The manner in which we welcome people.

comply ... garb Go through the actions which signify courteous behaviour.

extent Familiarity.

north-north-west On some occasions.

hawk A type of pickaxe, as well as a bird of prey.

Happily Perhaps.

individable That cannot be classified.

unlimited Including everything.

Seneca Roman dramatist, writer of tragedies.

Plautus Roman dramatist, writer of comedies.

treasure Before going to battle against the Ammonites Jephthah vowed that if victorious he would sacrifice to Jehovah whatever came first from his house to meet him on his return. He utterly defeated the Ammonites and on his return was first met by his only daughter, who acquiesced in the fulfilment of her father's rash vow. See Judges, 11,29–40.

as by lot A continuation of the ballad begun a few lines earlier.

valanced Covered with a beard.

nearer to heaven Taller.

chopine Heel of a lady's shoe. Hamlet comments on how much the boy who used to play the women's parts, has grown.

uncurrent Having no value.

cracked ... ring A piece of metal removed from inside the circle which surrounded the head of the sovereign on a coin; if the sovereign's head was clipped, the coin was no longer legal tender. The pun questions woman's virtue and taste.

caviare ... general i.e. too specialized to be enjoyed by the majority.

sallets Salads; also suggestive jokes.

more handsome ... fine More naturally constructed than artificially ornamented.

Aeneas' ... Dido Aeneas was one of the bravest of the Trojan warriors who managed to escape by sea when the city fell. On his travels he called at Carthage, where Dido, the Queen, fell so deeply in love with him that on his departure she had herself burnt to death on a funeral pyre.

Priam King of Troy, slain by Pyrrhus, one of the Greeks concealed in the wooden horse (see note on 'the ominous horse', over).

Hyrcanian beast Tiger.

ominous horse Wooden horse of Troy, a device used by the Greeks to get their warriors into the city they were besieging.

dismal Threatening.

total gules All in red (a heraldic term).

trick'd Marked out (another heraldic term).

impasted Dried to a paste.

o'ersized Covered over as with size (a kind of thick paste).

repugnant to In opposition to.

fell Cruel.

Ilium Troy.

stoops . . . base Falls.

like a neutral Indifferent.

matter Purpose.

against Before.

rack Clouds.

Cyclops Giants who worked as metal workers for Vulcan (Roman god of fire).

Mars's Roman god of war.

fellies Rims.

nave Hub.

Hecuba Priam's queen.

mobbled With muffled face.

bisson rheum Blinding tears.

clout Cloth.

o'erteemed Worn out with child-bearing.

milch Moist.

burning . . . heaven Stars.

abstract Summary.

God's bodkin By God's little body.

conceit Imagination.

function Activity.

horrid Terrifying.

muddy-mettled Dull-spirited.

peak Waste away.

John-a-dreams A dreaming weakling.

kindless Unnatural.

brave To be admired.

drab Whore.

scullion A kitchen servant.

tent Probe.

relative Unrelated.

Revision questions on Act II

1 Describe the character of Polonius in this act.
2 What function do the Players perform in this act?
3 What ideas does Hamlet express in the speech beginning 'I will tell you why', and ending 'Man delights not me', and how does he express those ideas?

Act III Scene 1

The King questions Rosencrantz and Guildenstern about Hamlet's state of mind; they have no news to ease his concern, but tell of the play to be performed in court that evening. The King and Polonius spy on a meeting between Hamlet and Ophelia. Hamlet is brutally offensive to Ophelia, who, after his departure, grieves over the change in him. The episode convinces the King that there may be some danger to himself from Hamlet, and he decides to send Hamlet on a diplomatic mission to England.

Commentary

The King's opening question sets a mood of uneasiness for the scene which is increased by the number of antitheses in the early speeches ('Niggard of question, but ... most free in his reply'). The conflicting tension between appearance and reality is dramatized by the spying figures watching Hamlet's meeting with Ophelia. It is given further emphasis through Polonius's words 'that with devotion's visage ... we do sugar o'er the devil himself.' The irony of this metaphor is made plain by Claudius's response, which picks up again the 'harlot' image which pervades the play. The audience is now aware of Claudius's guilt, which gives a dramatic emphasis to the following scene.

Conflict is revealed again by the opening lines of Hamlet's 'To be' speech of musing, and echoed in the imagery of war. His undecided state is shown in the many questions he asks. The speech ends on a note of tenderness; this is a moving moment in the play.

Hamlet puts on his 'irrational cap' again, and the language becomes prose and moves quickly, shifting suddenly through word associations from one idea to another and one image to

another, with the 'whore' theme running through everything.
The contrast between the innocence of Ophelia and the words
with which Hamlet addresses her gives dramatic power to the
innocence/guilt theme of the play.

Ophelia's emotion is shown in her cries to heaven to restore
Hamlet. Her soliloquy with its balanced phrases and rhythmical
form emphasizes the change in Hamlet from a man possessing
the perfect qualities of an Elizabethan gentleman, to the wild
figure on the stage. Her despair is revealed in all its depths by
her cry 'blasted with ecstacy'.

The final speeches of Claudius reveal his uneasiness in the
repeated negatives and the hatching egg metaphor. In his final
couplet he becomes again the public figure, his inner feelings
hidden.

drift of conference Roundabout way of talking.
assay him to Try to persuade him to take part in.
o'erraught Overtook.
content me Irony; Hamlet's interest in the Players will not please the
  King.
closely Privately.
Affront Meet face to face.
espials Spies.
Gracious This is addressed to the King.
colour . . . loneliness Provide a reason for your being alone.
rub Obstacle.
coil Turmoil; also circle of rope, a metaphor for all the troubles and
  experiences of life.
give . . . pause Make us hesitate.
contumely . . . dispriz'd Scorn . . . uncherished.
quietus Release.
bodkin Dagger.
fardels Burdens.
bourn Boundary.
native hue Red; the colour associated with resolution.
pale . . . thought Thought is associated with melancholy and is pale in
  colour.
pitch Height (a metaphor from falconry).
orisons Prayers.
honesty Straightforwardness; also chastity.
commerce Associations of trading and of sexual dealings.
inoculate Graft.
but . . . relish of it We shall still possess aspects of our former nature.
indifferent honest Fairly virtuous.

be thou Even though you be.
monsters Cuckolds.
paintings Make up.
mould of form i.e. fashion, appearance which others took as a model.
blown In full bloom.
hatch This develops the 'egg' metaphor begun with 'brood'.
tribute Payment.
fashion of himself His usual behaviour.
be round Speak bluntly.

Act III Scene 2

Hamlet instructs the Players on how they are to perform before the Court. He then speaks warmly to Horatio, praising his straightforwardness, and urges him to watch the King carefully during the performance. The Court enters, and Hamlet assumes his madness again, baiting Polonius and speaking suggestively to Ophelia. The play begins. The King expresses concern about its content, then orders it to end and leaves the room hastily, followed by the Court. The Queen sends for Hamlet, who is now convinced of the King's guilt. The scene ends with a soliloquy in which Hamlet sums up his courage and determines to face his mother.

Commentary

Hamlet speaks in prose to the Players, using more than once the word 'nature'. Natural feeling, natural behaviour, the truth, in contrast to what is artificial and false, is a recurring idea in the play, which is dramatized by the Players feigning the emotions they present on stage. It forms part of his praise for Horatio where words like 'flatter', 'candied', 'seeming', and references to clothes reinforce the theme.

Polonius's mention of the death of Caesar, the murder of an emperor, adds to the ominous atmosphere of the scene, and Hamlet's use of the word 'metal' continues the idea created in the blacksmith image. This in turn leads on to the imagery of the blackness of prostitution and infidelity.

The words of the 'Gonzalo' play explore further the themes of marital infidelity and murder for ambition. The language of the play is formal; the rhyming couplets and the word order give frequently a stilted, artificial and controlled effect, which contrasts with the passion and violence being expressed. The language becomes lyrical when the Player King falls asleep, creating a sense of peace, which is shattered by the entry of Lucianus. Claudius's instinctive, natural response to the speech and the violent activity which accompanies his departure from the scene, is striking after the static formality of the 'Gonzalo' play. The change in mood is emphasized by the short speeches, questions and short prose lines of Hamlet's excitement. By his references to the Catechism and to music Hamlet creates a sense that light has been shed upon the dark and evil deeds.

Hamlet's final soliloquy stands out strongly. The blank verse, in contrast to the prose which precedes it, renders the moment solemn. His horror emerges in the black associations of the imagery and in the violence and the unnaturalness: 'Now could I drink hot blood.' His emotion is expressed in his appeals to himself to carry through what he now knows he must do.

robustious Ranting.

Termagant A stock figure (representing a Saracen god) in the Mystery plays.

Herod Herod's massacre of the innocent children was a favourite subject for Mystery plays, in which Herod was presented as a violent, ranting character.

feature Appearance.

body Essence.

pressure Shape.

indifferently To a moderate extent.

barren Senseless.

As e'er . . . withal As I have ever met in my life.

pregnant Ready to act.

commeddled Mixed together.

occulted Hidden.

Vulcan See note p.34.

stithy Smithy.

chameleon's dish The chameleon was supposed to live on air.

country matters A pun on the first syllable, hence sexual innuendo.

sables A valuable dark fur.

hobby-horse A wicker horse fastened round the waist of a Morris dancer.

miching malicho Stealthy mischief.

naught Worthless, good-for-nothing. A much stronger word than the present-day 'naughty'.

Phoebus cart i.e. the sun.

Tellus The earth, the first being that sprang from Chaos.

Hymen The god of marriage.

in neither . . . extremity Women are either without love and fear, or experience an excess of both.

proof Experience.

operant Active.

still Always.

anchor Hermit.

tropically Figuratively (a 'trope' is a figure of speech).

galled jade Chafed horse.

dallying Moving (Hamlet is also referring to Claudius).

keen Sharp.

raven Supposedly a bird of ill-omen.

Confederate season A favourable opportunity.

Hecate The goddess of witchcraft.

extant Still in existence.

false fire A blank cartridge (the alliteration adds to the impact).

give o'er Put an end to.

turn Turk Treat badly.

Provincial roses Double roses (Fr. *Provençal*); as with the 'forest of feathers', Hamlet is referring to the extravagant dress worn by actors.

razed shoes Shoes on which leather is cut to form embroidery.

cry Company.

Damon Hamlet calls Horatio Damon in allusion to the famous friendship of Damon and Pythias, two Pythagorean philosophers. Hamlet's remark is thus a compliment to Horatio, implying that he holds him in the greatest esteem.

pajock A contemptible person.

perdie By God. Corruption of French *par dieu*.

choler Anger.

purgation Confession.

put . . . frame Talk sense.

these pickers and stealers Hamlet here holds up his hands. Cf. the phrase in the section of the Church Catechism dealing with our duty towards our neighbour, 'To keep my hands from picking and stealing.'

the proverb The proverb was, 'Whylst the grass doth growe, oft sterves the seely steede' – 'While waiting for the grass to grow the poor horse often dies.' Hamlet's meaning is, of course, that he may die before Claudius.

recover the wind Go to windward.

toil Net (these are both metaphors from hunting).

ventages The holes of the recorder.

to the top of my bent To the absolute limit (a metaphor from archery).

nature Natural feeling.
Nero The tyrannical Roman Emperor, who had his mother murdered for poisoning her husband. He was lustful, given to licentiousness and gluttony.
shent Rebuked.
give them seals Convert my words into actions.

Act III Scene 3

The King repeats to Rosencrantz and Guildenstern his determination to send Hamlet to England. Polonius states his intention of listening in to Hamlet's conversation with his mother. The King tries to pray, but finds that his guilt makes prayer impossible. Hamlet, who has encountered Claudius apparently at prayer, rejects the opportunity of killing him because, if he were killed at prayer, Claudius's sins would be forgiven and this would not satisfy Hamlet's thirst for revenge.

Commentary

After the previous public setting, this scene is private and intimate. Yet the sentiments expressed by the three figures on stage are public sentiments which disguise their true feelings. The opening speeches describe the power inherent in the King, and particularly how the well-being or weakness of the King affects his subjects. Placed at this point in the play, these sentiments have an ironic aspect. In these speeches Rosencrantz and Guildenstern emerge as flatterers. There is irony too in Polonius's remark that he will visit Claudius 'ere you go to bed'; Polonius will by that time be dead.

The mood changes, when Claudius is alone, to one of true intimacy. His speech reveals the conflict within him in its continual shifts from condemnation to forgiveness and mercy, from hell to heaven, from the red of blood to the white of snow. His longing for pardon is expressed through biblical references, and his anxiety is seen in the many questions. The alliteration of 'corrupted currents' gives emphasis to the image, which is further strengthened by the suggestion of falseness in 'gilded'. Claudius's self-honesty and acknowledged feelings of guilt present him in a more sympathetic light than before in the play.

Hamlet's speech is more nervous and tense than that of

Claudius, shown in the swift rhythms and short phrases following quickly one upon the other, and the references to excess and to food. The irony at this point is powerful; Hamlet does not kill Claudius because he is at prayer, yet the audience knows that Claudius cannot pray.

the terms ... estate My position as King.
peculiar Individual.
noyance Harm.
cess Death.
gulf Whirlpool.
tax him home Reproach him thoroughly.
of vantage In addition.
It hath ... murder A reference to the murder of Abel by Cain in Genesis 4, 1–15.
shuffling Avoidance by deceit.
limed Referring to an old method of catching birds by spreading on twigs a sticky substance called bird-lime.
That ... scann'd That needs looking into.
grossly ... bread For worldly reward (the 'food' image is repeated in 'season'd').
broad blown In full bloom.
flush Full of life.
in our circumstance As it seems to us.
fit and season'd Fully prepared.
hent Opportunity.

Act III Scene 4

Polonius, with the Queen's agreement, hides behind an arras in her room as Hamlet enters. Hamlet's words frighten her, so that Polonius calls out. Hamlet stabs him through the arras, believing him to be Claudius. Hamlet then compares his father with Claudius and wildly condemns his mother for her sexual relationship with Claudius. The Ghost appears, seen only by Hamlet, and urges him not to forget to avenge his murder, but to deal kindly with his mother. This occurrence convinces his mother that Hamlet is mad, an accusation which Hamlet rejects, urging her to confess her part in the murder, and to abstain from sexual relations with Claudius. Hamlet leaves to drag Polonius's body into a neighbouring room.

Commentary

Polonius's opening words contain a double irony in the phrase 'I'll silence me even here'; not only are the words followed by more from the loquacious Polonius, but it also anticipates his imminent death, brought about by his inability to keep quiet.

The tension between Hamlet and his mother is revealed through the single line speeches and Hamlet's insulting repetition of his mother's words. The lines become very fragmented, reflecting the confusion that arises from the Queen's misunderstanding of Hamlet's words 'Where you may see the inmost part of you'; the Queen's fear that he intends to murder her introduces the idea of violence, which is then enacted dramatically in the killing of Polonius, an event which also dramatizes the confusion at this point in the play.

Hamlet's condemnation of his mother is made vivid by the imagery of war and prostitution that pervades it. He contrasts the two Kings strongly, depicting his father in terms of the greatest classical gods, and Claudius in terms of darkness, disease and corruption. The contrast of past and present, 'here was' . . . 'here is', intensifies the difference between the two men. The second part of the speech centres upon his mother's sexual activity. Hamlet's horror is revealed through expressions like 'rank sweat', 'enseamed bed', 'nasty sty', and reaches a climax in the metaphor of a 'cutpurse' stealing 'the precious diadem'; these final words epitomize Hamlet's feelings about his mother and recall her position as Queen.

The atmosphere of fear is heightened by the appearance of the Ghost; this section of the scene has an added dramatic effect in that the visibility of the Ghost to Hamlet and not to the Queen acts as a stage metaphor for the seeing of truth in the play. The portraits and the mirror also contribute to the exploration of this theme of seeing clearly.

Hamlet's final speech gives us his opinion of Rosencrantz and Guildenstern, and shows his determination and his ability now to see clearly what is, rather than what seems to be.

be round Speak plainly to him.
busy Meddlesome.
braz'd Covered with brass.
contraction The sweating of a contract.

rhapsody A meaningless string.

solidity . . . mass Earth.

tristful Sad (Fr. *triste*).

as against . . . doom As if ready for the day of judgement.

thought-sick Sick with anxiety.

the index This was formerly placed at the beginning of a book.

counterfeit presentment Portrait.

station Way of standing.

Mercury Roman messenger of the gods.

batten Fatten.

blood Sexual desire.

sense The senses.

cozen'd Deceived.

hoodman-blind Blind man's buff.

sans Without (Fr.).

mope Be so unaware.

mutine Rebel.

frost . . . burn The antithesis underlines his words.

panders will Is used to justify passion.

grained Engrained.

tinct Colour.

enseamed Soaked in grease (a metaphor from falconry).

a vice of kings *Vice* was a conventional character of morality plays (in which the characters were various qualities, e.g. *Pride*, *Ambition*).

of shreds and patches Continuing the idea of 'a vice of kings' – a mere clown of a king, referring to the motley dress of the professional jester.

life in excrements Hair and nails were called excrements in Elizabethan English.

capable i.e. of feeling.

effects Planned deeds.

want true colour Be presented in a false light.

skin and film Cover over (the disease metaphor is developed).

pursy Bloated.

who . . . evil Who eats away all consciousness of the evil we habitually commit.

their This refers to 'heaven'.

reechy Foul.

paddock Toad.

gib Tom-cat.

conclusions Experiments (in trying to fly).

marshal Conduct.

Hoist . . . petard Blown up with his own bomb.

Revision questions on Act III

1 Discuss the dramatic importance of the Players in Act III.
2 Analyse fully Hamlet's 'To be' speech in Scene 1.
3 Analyse the character and importance of Ophelia in Act III.
4 Consider the roles of Claudius and Gertrude in this Act.
5 Discuss the use of (a) sexual or (b) disease or (c) war imagery in Act III.

Act IV Scene 1

The Queen explains to Claudius that Hamlet has killed Polonius. Claudius realizes that he might have been killed in Polonius's place. He fears the repercussions the murder might have, and resolves to send Hamlet to England immediately.

Commentary

The Queen describes how serious she thinks Hamlet's madness is. Her first speech ends with words of simplicity and long vowels which show her affection for the dead Polonius.

Claudius's speech is loaded with justification for his own actions, and is an effort to whitewash his name, thus dispelling the audience's new-found sympathy. He uses imagery of disease and warfare, which contrasts with Gertrude's description of Hamlet in terms of precious gold. She concentrates her concern on Hamlet, Claudius his concern on himself. The alliteration of 's' in the final line of the scene emphasizes his worry at the way events are going.

brainish Frenzied.
short Within bounds.
out of haunt In seclusion.
divulging Being revealed to the world.
ore i.e. gold ore.
mineral i.e. mine.
level Straight.
blank Target.

Act IV Scene 2

Rosencrantz and Guildenstern ask Hamlet where he has put Polonius's body; Hamlet answers in riddles.

Commentary

The confusion of Hamlet's apparent madness contains great sense. In his play on 'sponge' and his remark about the ape he makes it clear he is aware of the true natures of both Rosencrantz and Guildenstern, and of Claudius.

safely stowed Hamlet is referring to the body of Polonius.
keep your counsel Keep your secrets.
replication Answer.
countenance Favour.
like an ape ... swallowed Apes have a pouch on each side of the jaw in which they keep the food they have first put in their mouth, until all the rest has been eaten.
body ... King ... body Hamlet is saying that the body is in the palace with the King, but the King is not dead like the body; this is typical of his word-play in his 'madness'.

Act IV Scene 3

The King repeats how dangerous Hamlet is to the State, but says that he must act carefully because of Hamlet's popularity with the people. He tells Hamlet that for his own safety he must go to England. Hamlet, talking in apparent riddles, reveals where Polonius's body lies. The King urges Rosencrantz and Guildenstern to make sure Hamlet is quickly got on board the ship for England, and in a final soliloquy reveals that the letters accompanying Hamlet are to bring about his death.

Commentary

The King continues to be devious in what he says, a fact which is shown in the word 'seem'. By repeating 'desperate' he makes plain his fear of Hamlet; the final couplet of his soliloquy puts further emphasis on this.

Hamlet's language is again full of puns, which bring out the common nature of all men, both King and beggar. The image of the worm suggests corruption and destructiveness, and explores further the theme that the whole state is affected by the actions of the King.

distracted Fickle.

scourge Punishment.

deliberate pause A considered judgement (something that has been deliberated upon and paused over).

appliance Remedy.

politic worms No doubt alluding to the famous Diet of Worms (1521) at which Luther defended his doctrines before the Emperor Charles and the Church assembly. The Diet was regarded by Protestants as an assembly of politicians.

variable service Different courses.

do tender Have concern for.

tend Wait.

I see a cherub . . . them Hamlet hints that he has an idea of what the King is planning. A cherub was supposed to be able to see the truth.

at foot Close behind.

leans on Concerns.

set Value.

process Mandate.

Howe'er . . . joys Nothing that happens gives me joy.

Act IV Scene 4

Hamlet, taking his departure, meets Fortinbras's army on its way to Poland. Their willingness to risk their lives for apparently so little, causes Hamlet, in a soliloquy, to consider man's ability to reason, and his own inaction.

Commentary

This scene is one of incipient action and is important for the plot in that it prepares for the arrival of Fortinbras at the end of the play. The factual nature of the conversation with the Captain contrasts with the poetic language of Hamlet's reasoning in his soliloquy, underlining Hamlet's thoughtful nature, which hesitates before action. The contrast is enhanced and related to Hamlet's internal conflict by his contrasting Fortinbras with himself, and by the antitheses of 'beast' and 'godlike', 'mass and charge' and 'delicate and tender'. The speech forms a rational argument which builds to a climax as Hamlet lists the reasons for him to act, made vivid by words connected with death. Hamlet's final couplet expresses his determination to carry out his revenge.

conveyance of Escort for.
main The mainland (the main part of the country).
farm Lease.
ranker rate Higher value.
in fee Outright.
debate . . . straw Hamlet is amazed at the resources employed for such a small portion of land.
impostume Abscess.
discourse Ability to reason.
fust Grow musty.
event Outcome.
Makes mouths at Is contemptuous of.
fantasy Illusion.
trick Trifle.
Whereon . . . try Too small to contain those fighting for.
continent Container.

Act IV Scene 5

The Queen agrees unwillingly to speak with Ophelia, whose irrational behaviour and incoherent speech shock the King; he attributes it to her father's death. Laertes arrives, threatening violence against the King and demanding an explanation for his father's death and hasty burial. His passion increases when he sees Ophelia's state. The King takes him away to talk with him.

Commentary

The Queen's emotion is shown in the opening lines through the simple language of her short sentences; in her brief soliloquy before Ophelia's entry she reveals her sense of guilt, which intensifies the tragedy of Ophelia's innocent suffering. The repetition of the words 'spill', 'spilt', indicates her knowledge that the truth will be brought into the open, and increases the audience's sense that the play is approaching its climax.

The Gentleman's speech prepares the audience for the entry of Ophelia and sets the emotional mood of the scene. Ophelia's entry heightens the emotion; she is changed greatly from her previous character, and this change dramatizes the effects of the evil in the play. It is emphasized by the almost childlike simplicity of her language, by the short songs, the imagery of death and love, and by the purity suggested by flowers, grass and snow. The tragedy of destroyed innocence is underlined, as her language begins to include sexual innuendo and, in the 'By Gis' song, the exploitation of innocence.

The mood changes abruptly, on her departure, with the King's speech; his opening words are in the form of a proverb which states generalities and hides the truth. The war imagery which runs through his speech echoes the violence, emanating from his actions, which has affected Ophelia. His own responsibility, which he attempts to avoid, is underlined in the irony of his word 'beast'.

The significance of Laertes's return is illustrated by the metaphor of the sea flooding the land. His vigour and hot temper is made clear in the violence and swiftly moving lines of his speeches, and his reference to revenge recalls the parallel between him and Hamlet. His openness and excitement emphasize the controlled nature of the King, who takes refuge in his kingship 'There's such divinity doth hedge a king.' Throughout the verbal conflict between Laertes and the King there is a strong hint that Claudius's power is on the wane; this reaches its culmination in Laertes's simile of 'the king, life-rend'ring pelican' with its suggestion that a new beginning is approaching, nourished by Laertes's blood.

The scene ends with the irony of the King's final line: 'Where the offence is, let the great axe fall.'

distract Mad.
Spurns . . . at straws Objects angrily to unimportant matters.
to collection To an understanding of some meaning.
aim Guess.
yield Represent.
unhappily Mischievously.
amiss Misfortune.
cockle hat A hat bearing a cockle shell as a badge indicating that the wearer had been on a pilgrimage to a holy shrine, in particular the shrine of St James of Compostella in Spain.
shoon Shoes (with the staff, these were also symbols of the pilgrim;

lovers were traditionally associated in literature with pilgrims).

Larded Decorated.

good dild you God reward you.

owl . . . baker's daughter A possible allusion to the story of a baker's daughter who was turned into an owl for refusing to give bread to Christ.

Conceit Brooding.

Gis Probably a corruption of Jesus.

Cock A corruption of God; also, phallus.

muddied Confused.

greenly Unwisely.

In hugger-mugger In secret haste.

wonder Bewilderment.

in clouds Confused.

wants not buzzers Does not lack gossips.

of matter beggar'd Short of factual information.

will nothing stick Will not hesitate.

a murd'ring piece A type of cannon loaded with many small pieces of shot.

superfluous i.e. many are killed unnecessarily.

Switzers Royal guards. The Swiss were the mercenary soldiers of Europe.

overpeering Exceeding.

list Boundary.

flats Flat land.

in a riotous head With a riotous mob.

word Maxim.

counter In the opposite direction (a metaphor from hunting).

cuckold The husband of a wife who has committed adultery.

fear Fear for.

both the worlds . . . negligence I am neither concerned about my life now nor after death.

swoopstake i.e. indiscriminately.

pelican The pelican is supposed to tear open its own breast to feed its young with its own blood.

sensibly Full of feeling.

'pear Appear.

virtue Power.

turn the beam Turn the bar of the balance.

fine Delicate.

instance Sample.

wheel Refrain.

this nothing's . . . matter This nonsense conveys more than sense would convey.

document Lesson.

fennel ... columbines Flowers symbolizing infidelity in marriage; obviously presented to the Queen.
rue Flower symbolizing sorrow and repentance.
daisy Flower symbolizing unhappy love.
violets Flowers symbolizing faithfulness.
poll Head (the song refers to the dead Polonius, and to the loss of innocence).
Or Unless.
touch'd Implicated.
hatchment Coat of arms.

Act IV Scene 6

Horatio receives a letter from some sailors, sent by Hamlet, and conveys other letters to the King.

Commentary

This short scene takes the plot forward and adds to the suspense. It continues the sense of action begun with Laertes in the previous scene.

overlooked Perused.
appointment Equipment.
thieves of mercy Merciful thieves (with an association with 'angels of mercy', suggesting Hamlet's rescue from death).
a turn A good turn.
bore Part of a gun; here it means 'importance'.

Act IV Scene 7

Letters are brought to the King from Hamlet announcing his return to Denmark. Laertes, having been persuaded by the King that Hamlet was responsible for his father's death, expresses his strong desire for revenge. Encouraged by the King he plots to kill Hamlet using a poisoned rapier in a fencing duel.

Commentary

The King's speech to Laertes again illustrates his devious nature. In contrast to Laertes's brief remarks, the length of the King's speeches, his carefully constructed arguments, his flattery of

Laertes through his remembrance of Lamord, support the picture of his corrupt nature. This is an intimate and private scene, and provides information which affects the audience's sympathies in the final scene of the play.

The Queen's account of Ophelia's death creates a moving and tragic moment which contrasts strongly with the corruption that has just been witnessed. Again the flowers, the water, the songs, the shepherds and the 'cold maids' present images of innocence and purity, which have been sullied and destroyed.

knowing Knowledgeable.
feats Evil deeds.
capital Deserving death.
mainly Strongly.
unsinew'd Weak.
conjunctive to Closely connected to.
sphere Orbit.
count Accounting.
general gender Common sort (of people).
spring . . . stone i.e. because of the high lime content of the water.
gyves Fetters, i.e. bad qualities (Claudius uses a sequence of images here).
challenger on mount Supreme challenger.
naked Without any belongings.
abuse Deception.
devise me Make it clear to me.
checking at Turning aside from.
uncharge the practice Acquit us of the plot.
siege Rank.
weeds Sober clothes.
been incorps'd Become part of the body.
demi natur'd Taken on half the nature.
topp'd my thought Surpassed what I thought was possible.
forgery . . . shapes and tricks Imagination of figures and skilful deeds.
made confession of Gave good report of.
defence Swordsmanship.
scrimers fencers.
passages of proof Proved circumstances.
pleurisy Excess.
That we would do What we would do.
quick Sensitive part.
in fine In the end.
remiss Trustful.
unbated Unblunted.

mountebank Quack, a fake.
cataplasm Plaster.
simples Medicinal herbs.
under the moon Herbs gathered by moonlight were supposed to have greater power.
gall Scratch.
our shape The part we are to play.
drift Scheme.
blast in proof Break down in performance.
for the nonce For the occasion.
stuck Sword thrust.
askant Across.
hoary Silver grey.
crow-flowers Ragged robins.
long purples A type of wild orchis.
liberal Free-speaking.
cold Chaste.
crownet Formed into a wreath.
envious Malicious.
lauds Songs.
incapable Unaware.
Indued unto Adapted to.
trick Way, custom.
the woman . . . out The woman (weakness) will be out of me.
douts Drowns.

Revision questions on Act IV

1 In what ways does Laertes resemble his father?
2 What is the dramatic function of Ophelia in this Act?
3 Analyse the ideas and the language of Hamlet's 'How all occasions' speech in Scene 4.
4 What does this Act contribute to the final outcome of the play?

Act V Scene 1

Hamlet and Horatio come upon two Gravediggers preparing a grave. The skulls they throw up lead Hamlet to reflect upon human destiny. The arrival of the funeral party reveals the grave to be that of Ophelia, and the words of the Priest suggest that her death was suicide. Laertes leaps into the grave for a final farewell to Ophelia, whereupon Hamlet joins him and grapples with him. They are separated. The scene ends with the King reminding Laertes of their plan.

Commentary

The graveyard setting for this scene enhances a sense of impending tragedy, and this is intensified by the theme of death in the language, by the skulls on stage, and by the suggestion of suicide in the Gravedigger's opening speech. The warmth and humour of the Gravediggers, and the wit and confusion of their language, give a lightness to this moment in the play, which at the same time increases the tragedy. Death is made an inevitable and everyday event, one which reduces all human beings to the same level. The quality of language seems superficial, but reaches a profundity through puns and word associations, which Hamlet carries on in his reflections on the value of human endeavour and weakness, expressed in a series of rhetorical questions. The ease with which Hamlet talks to the Gravediggers underlines his humanity and his lack of pride and superiority, and strengthens the audience's sympathy for him. This sympathy is increased as Hamlet recalls Yorick, and his pleasure at the memory emphasizes by contrast the horror of the present.

The mood of the scene changes just before the arrival of the funeral party, with a shift from prose to blank verse. A sense of innocence and purity appears again in the play with the flowers and the use of words like 'virgin' and 'maiden', and it is given solemnity by the ceremony and the Priest. The destruction of this innocence is shown powerfully with the appearance of Ophelia's dead body and by the poetic speeches of Laertes and the Queen, which form a poignant moment in the scene. This is contributed to by the brief, simple exclamation of Hamlet when he realizes whose grave it is.

The explosion of emotion that follows is expressed in the magnitude and excess of the imagery, in the swift rhythms and quick interchange of speeches, and the scuffle in the grave. The violence is ended by the Queen's beautiful simile of the 'dove', which gives a hint of the peace which will end the corruption and the tragedy.

wilfully Note that the Queen had not suggested before that Ophelia had committed suicide.

se offendendo Se defendendo (the Clown's mistake), in self-defence.

argal A mispronunciation of *ergo* – therefore.

Delver Digger.

quest Inquest.

countenance Permission.

even-Christian Fellow Christian.

unyoke That's an end of it.

stoup Flagon.

behove Advantage.

property of easiness Easy job (i.e. he has become used to it).

hath the daintier sense Is more sensitive.

jowls Throws.

o'er offices Exercises his authority over.

chopless Without a jaw.

mazard head.

here's fine revolution i.e. it has come round (revolved) to this.

trick Ability.

loggets Shaped pieces of wood. The game consisted in tossing the loggets at a stake fixed in the ground.

for and And also.

quiddities/quillities Quibbling presentation of detail.

sconce Head.

action of battery Summons for assault.

statutes . . . recognizances Legal terms used in the purchase of land.

fines . . . recoveries Legal terms used in converting an entailed estate for sale.

double vouchers Where two people vouch for the tenant's title.

the fine The end result.

indentures Duplicates of a deed.

assurance A pun on the ordinary sense; and a deed written on parchment.

quick Living.

absolute Particular.

by the card Exactly.

picked Refined.

kibe A sore place on the heel.

hold Wait for.

lay in Laying in the ground.

whoreson A familiar expression expressing contempt.

fancy Imagination.

paint an inch thick A literary reference to a type of dance in which a skull appeared before a lady getting up and preparing her hair and face for the day. It continues the 'whore' image of the play.

favour Face.

too curiously In too much detail.
likelihood to lead it i.e. it is not too far fetched to imagine that this
  would be likely to happen.
flaw Sudden gust of wind.
maimed Incomplete.
estate High rank.
Couch we Let us hide.
warranty Permission.
doubtful Suspicious.
shards Fragments of broken pottery.
crants Garlands.
strewments Flowers scattered on the grave.
sage Solemn.
ingenious sense Alert mind.
Pelion; Olympus; Ossa Mountains in Greece. Olympus was the home
  of the gods.
splenative Hot tempered.
eisel Vinegar.
mouth Speak.
present push Immediate test.

Act V Scene 2

Hamlet relates to Horatio his discovery of the plot to kill him in
England, and how he rewrote the letters ordering the death of
Rosencrantz and Guildenstern, before escaping to Denmark on
the pirate ship. Osric brings a message from the King detailing
the duel between Hamlet and Laertes. The Court enters, Hamlet speaks warmly to Laertes, attributing his previous behaviour
to his own madness. The King secretly poisons a cup of wine,
and the duel begins. The Queen drinks the poisoned wine.
Laertes wounds Hamlet, they exchange rapiers in the scuffle
and Hamlet wounds Laertes. The Queen dies. Laertes tells
Hamlet that the rapier is poisoned, whereupon Hamlet wounds
the King, who dies; this is quickly followed by Laertes's death.
Fortinbras enters from Poland and is elected heir to Hamlet,
who then dies himself. The play ends with praise of Hamlet by
Horatio and Fortinbras.

Commentary

The mood of conspiracy and corruption is continued in this
scene by Hamlet's account of the letters. Horatio's role is to

prompt Hamlet to give this necessary information to the audience. The conversation moves to the King, and Osric enters, dramatizing the state of the Court under Claudius. His dress and his flattery of Laertes epitomize the exaggeration and flattery which dominate the Court, with the repetition of 'very' and 'most' and the numerous 's' sounds underlining this. Hamlet's scorn of Osric, his imitation of his phrases, emphasize this even more, and m..ke Hamlet stand out as representing opposite values, while the references to weapons set the tone for the violence that is to come.

Hamlet's madness speech and Laertes's reply create a pause in the swift flow of the scene, a moment of forgiving before the tragic action begins; the 'star' simile illustrates both the quality of Hamlet and Laertes in contrast to the villainy of the rest of the Court, and the immensity of the violence that is to come. The scene slows again as Claudius poisons the wine, drawing attention to his act; his use of the word 'union' reflects ironically on the poisoning, and by means of a pun on marriage union extends his words to comment on the whole action of the play.

The short lines of the following speeches increase the sense of action in the scene until the participants are wounded. Laertes's speech, with its repetition of words associated with treachery, sums up the corruption that has led to this moment and forms a contrast to Horatio's final words to Hamlet; his reference to 'angels' and 'music' creates a feeling of Hamlet's essential goodness, a feeling too that the time of evil is now past, and looks forward to a more harmonious future. The entry of Fortinbras reinforces this sense of a new future; his final words of praise for Hamlet as the bodies are carried off the stage form a final and moving climax to the end of the play.

bilboes Shackles.
learn i.e. teach.
in fine Finally.
Larded Decorated.
in my life If I were allowed to live.
on the supervise On reading it through.
no leisure bated No time intervening.
I . . . play Before I had decided what action to take my brain had set to work (a metaphor from the stage).
statists Statesmen.

comma A hardly perceptible interference.
charge Importance.
shriving-time Time for confession.
ordinant In command of events.
model Replica.
subscrib'd Signed.
go to it Go to their death.
insinuation Interfering.
pass Sword-thrust.
fell See note p.34.
stand . . . upon Does it not now put the responsibility on me.
election i.e. the throne.
angle Hook (in fishing).
proper Own.
coz'nage Deception.
image . . . cause Both Hamlet's and Laertes's fathers have been
  murdered.
bravery Flaunting nature.
crib Food box.
mess Table.
chaff Rough country fellow.
dirt Land.
complexion Disposition.
absolute Perfect.
differences Unusual quantities.
soft society Good breeding.
feelingly Justly.
card of calendar Model.
continent Embodiment.
definement Description.
perdition Loss.
dozy Make dizzy.
yaw Make a crooked course.
in respect of In comparison with.
article i.e. importance.
infusion Essential quality.
dearth Value.
his semblable . . . mirror There is no-one else like him.
trace . . . umbrage Keep pace with his shadow.
concernancy Of what concern is it to us.
more rawer breath Cruder speech.
imputation Value.
in his meed In his service.
impawned Pledged.
their assigns What goes with them.

hanger A strap by which the rapier or poniard was attached to the girdle.

very responsive to Close in design to.

liberal conceit Rich decoration.

margin Marginal note.

german Fitting.

breathing time Time for exercise.

lapwing . . . head i.e. is only just hatched – a reference to Osric's youthful pretensions.

comply with Pay formal compliments to.

drossy Lacking in seriousness.

time Fashion.

out of an habit of encounter From frequent contact.

yeasty Frothy.

out Burst.

use . . . entertainment Make a courteous gesture.

gaingiving Misgiving.

tis . . . to come It is not in the future.

of aught . . . aught Knows anything about what he leaves behind.

betimes Early.

this presence Those present.

exception Disapproval.

voice . . . precedent Authoritative opinion, justified by precedent.

ungor'd Unsullied.

foil A pun on the meaning; a setting for a jewel which shows it off to advantage.

stick fiery off Stand out brightly.

quit Equalize.

union Pearl.

kettle Kettle-drum, made by stretching a skin over a copper drum.

fat Sweaty.

make a wanton of me Trifle with me.

springe Snare.

unbated Unblunted.

practice Deception.

union Pun on marriage union and pearl (see above).

mutes Actors who have no speaking parts; onlookers.

I am . . . antique Roman I prefer suicide.

a Dane One who leads an unworthy life.

o'ercrows Subdues (a metaphor from cock fighting).

occurrents Occurrences.

This quarry This pile of dead bodies.

cries on havoc Cries aloud indiscriminate slaughter (a metaphor from hunting).

toward In preparation.

jump See note p.16.

carnal Incestuous.
put on Brought about.
of memory Remembered.
put on Put to the test.

Revision questions on Act V

1 Explain the importance of the Gravedigger's scene at this point in the play.

2 Discuss Hamlet's conversation with Osric, and show the significance of Osric in this act.

3 Describe the events leading up to the death of Hamlet in Scene 2 of this act.

4 Discuss the importance of the events and conversations that happen after the death of Hamlet.

5 Write an essay on Shakespeare's use of contrast in this act.

General questions

1 What is the importance of the Ghost in the play?
2 Compare and contrast the figures of Hamlet and Laertes.
3 What is the importance of Hamlet's soliloquies in the play?
4 Describe the graveyard scene, and show its importance in the play.
5 Examine how Shakespeare uses disease imagery and flowers in the play.
6 How far do you consider Hamlet to be mad?
7 Examine in detail the scene between Hamlet and his mother, and show its importance in the play.
8 How far do you consider Hamlet to be unable to make up his mind?
9 What does Polonius contribute to the play?
10 How important is Ophelia in the play?
11 Horatio's only function is to enable factual information to be given to the audience. Discuss this statement.
12 Select one soliloquy in the play and analyse the ideas and the language.
13 How much does Hamlet love Ophelia? Discuss the functions of this love in the play.
14 Compare and contrast Horatio with Rosencrantz and Guildenstern.
15 Discuss the dramatic qualities of one of the scenes in which Ophelia appears mad.
16 There are too many problems in *Hamlet* for the play to be successfully staged. Discuss two problems of the play in the light of this statement.
17 What qualities in *Hamlet* make the play a tragedy?
18 How far is the Queen a tragic figure?
19 Write an essay on the use of poetry and prose in *Hamlet*.
20 Indicate the range of humour used by Shakespeare in *Hamlet*.

Note style answer

1 What is the importance of the Ghost in the play?

(a) To give information: (I,5) about the murder – Ghost's own words – the knowledge affects the way Claudius is viewed.

(b) To create atmosphere: (I,1+4+5) fear – horror – death; 'this thing', 'dreaded sight'. Talked about before it appears.
   Link with themes through language:
(*i*)   violence – warlike appearance, armour, martial stalk (I,1).
(*ii*)   foreboding – evil to state (I,1 Horatio), omen (I,1 Horatio).
(*iii*)   disorder – Julius Caesar (I,1 Horatio); 'freeze young blood', 'eyes start from spheres' (I,5 Ghost).
(*iv*)   secrecy – silence (I,1 Horatio).

(c) Symbol of goodness – the dead Hamlet embodiment of kingly virtue: 'valient' (I,1 Horatio), 'goodly king' (I,1 Horatio), 'excellent' (I,2 Hamlet), Hyperion, Jove etc. (III,4 Hamlet).
   Dramatic contrast to Claudius: 'revelry' (I,4 Hamlet), Hyperion/satyr (I,2 Hamlet), portraits of both (III,4 Hamlet), goodness corrupted by evil (I,5 blood/poison, polluted milk).

(d) Good/evil uncertainty: 'spirit of health or goblin damned' (I,4 Hamlet).

Shakespeare's art in *Hamlet*
Setting

Hamlet portrays events in the Danish royal family, and in keeping with a Danish setting Shakespeare has given a romantic colouring to a play of violence and revenge. The castle of Elsinor, the names of Hamlet, Gertrude, Fortinbras, Rosencrantz and Guildenstern, the talk of preparations for war between Denmark and Norway, the episode in which Fortinbras's army crosses Denmark on its way to Poland, all give an authentic Danish flavour to the play. This is increased by references within the play to Danish customs, the King's 'rouse', the 'Rhenish wine' that he drinks, the 'kettle-drum and trumpet' that accompany his feasting.

The physical setting of the play and the references to Danish customs cannot, however, disguise the fact that the play is essentially English. The language is that of Elizabethan England, and so are many of the incidents and references.

The theatrical detail in the play, and the travelling players who arrive at Court, belong to those groups of English players with whom Shakespeare was so familiar. Their clothes, the 'forest of feathers', the 'razed shoes', the 'periwig-pated fellow', and Hamlet's criticism of the way players 'mouth' and 'tear a passion to tatters' and 'strutted and bellowed', refer to English players. Mention of the 'groundlings', and of the roof of the Globe Theatre, 'this majestical roof fretted with golden fire' add to the English flavour. Shakespeare is furthermore topical in his reference to 'an eyrie of children, little eyases', the boy players who had recently become popular at the Blackfriars Theatre, and whose popularity forced adult companies to become travelling players.

Ophelia's description of Hamlet as he used to be, 'courtier, scholar, soldier, . . . rose of the fair state, . . . glass of fashion', is a vivid portrayal of an Elizabethan courtier. The songs that she sings in her madness were familiar English songs of the period, and the 'recorder' and 'pipe' that Hamlet mentions were popular instruments of the time. The churchyards have an English flavour, and the 'town crier' and 'journeyman', the 'drab' and 'scullion', were familiar figures in English life.

Above all, the flowers which Ophelia offers, daisy, violets, rosemary, pansies, fennel, columbine, rue, were typical flowers of the English countryside; and the Queen's description of her death, the brook, the willow, the 'crow flowers, nettles, daisies and long purples' create a setting that is pure Elizabethan England.

Themes

The most obvious theme of the play is that of revenge: the Ghost's demand that Hamlet should avenge his murder, and Hamlet's struggles with the charge and eventual success in achieving it. The theme is reinforced by Laertes's determination to avenge his father's death by killing Hamlet.

Within the play other themes are explored too. Closely connected with the murder of Hamlet, Shakespeare debates the question which has much interested him in other plays, that is, the effects of the murder of a king or ruler upon the state. The outcome of such an act is raised in the opening scene by Horatio, Marcellus and Bernardo. They are unaware that Hamlet has been murdered, but their comparisons of the preparations for war in Denmark and the appearance of the Ghost, with the disastrous and terrifying events that followed the death of Julius Caesar, make the question relevant. The opening scenes make absolutely clear that the death of the King and the Queen's hasty remarriage to Claudius are having a disastrous effect upon the whole state of Denmark; this is shown in Hamlet's reference to the poor reputation Denmark is gaining abroad (I,4). Hamlet's comment that 'the time is out of joint' (I,5) and Marcellus's statement that 'something is rotten in the state of Denmark' (I,4) are explicit.

Corruption is another theme explored in the play. Claudius's murder of old Hamlet for his own ambition and his plan to kill young Hamlet when he becomes aware of the crime is one aspect of the treatment of this theme. Much more attention, however, is given to the Queen's remarriage and the corrupt, incestuous quality of her relationship with Claudius. The imagery that Hamlet uses to describe his mother's remarriage is violent, associated with disease, prostitution and filth.

The theme of corruption is extended further in the play through other characters. Polonius's spying on Laertes, on Hamlet and Ophelia, on Hamlet and Gertrude, is shown to be wrong through Hamlet's comments and Polonius's ignominious death. The theme is developed through Rosencrantz and Guildenstern, brought to Court solely to try to find out what is troubling Hamlet; it is demonstrated by their flattery of Claudius, by their involvement in the plot to kill Hamlet and their deaths as a result of their own treachery. The corruption involved in flattery is picked up in Osric, and is also extended with the treatment of Laertes who, through flattery, is persuaded by Claudius to act dishonourably in the duel with Hamlet.

The play also treats in depth the theme of the reflective personality, contrasting it with the active personality. Hamlet's inability to carry out the revenge is partly caused by his need for certainty about Claudius's guilt and, once certain of this, his need for the right opportunity. It is also caused by his repulsion for such a deed. By nature he is reflective and thoughtful, as his many long soliloquies show. He is interested in the nature of human reason, in how this distinguishes human beings from animals, and what responsibilities it puts upon human beings. He is also interested in death, in the meaning of death and in what awaits human beings after life. His metaphysical considerations about death pervade the whole play, and are given dramatic form through the scenes with the Ghost and the scene in the churchyard, and made vivid through the imagery associated with death and particularly with Hell.

Revenge tragedy

Revenge tragedy received its inspiration from Seneca, a Roman writer whose work insisted upon the triumph of moral law, and was packed with acts of revenge which were violent, cruel, and involved much bloodshed. The horror was increased by ghost scenes and scenes of madness. The revenger usually died in carrying out the revenge.

One of the earliest English examples of revenge tragedy was

The Spanish Tragedy, written by Thomas Kyd, probably in 1588. The genre remained popular throughout the late sixteenth century, and flowered in the early seventeenth century with the work of Webster, Middleton and Tourneur.

The plays balance corruption, vice and evil, with moral retribution, and the irrational, shown explicitly in the mad scenes, with rational thinking and a longing for justice.

Another feature of revenge tragedy is the melancholy revenger, seen to a certain extent in Hamlet, and much more clearly in the Jacobean plays. The model for this figure was found in the work of Machiavelli (1469–1527) the celebrated Florentine statesman noted for his writings on political philosophy.

The characters

Hamlet

O cursed spite,
That ever I was born to set it right. (I,5)

Hamlet is first mentioned in the play by Horatio who refers to him in terms of 'love' and 'duty'. Horatio is respected for his sense of honour and his commonsense and also as a friend of Hamlet. This gives a favourable impression of Hamlet at the beginning of the play.

Hamlet's first appearance is in the Court scene where his mourning clothes make him conspicuous among the other people. He is depressed and clearly antagonistic towards the King. His first soliloquy reveals the depth of his sorrow to be such as to make suicide an attractive proposition; it also reveals his horror at his mother's hasty remarriage to a man whom he finds so much inferior to his own dead father. Hamlet is conscious that out of such an act, only misfortune can emerge. He also voices his disgust at the King's indulgence in drinking and feasting, and his fears for Denmark's reputation.

Hamlet's reflections on the 'vicious mole of nature' in some people (I,4) show his thoughtfulness, his interest in considering the state of humankind and, as later speeches show, human destiny. His sensitivity is plain in his horror at the appearance of the Ghost and his immediate questioning of its implications. Yet Hamlet possesses the courage to follow it, and his bravery is emphasized by the fear of his companions and their advice that he should not do so.

His courage is shown again, and his sense of duty, in his immediate agreement to the Ghost's request that he should avenge his father's death. Yet the shock of the revelation affects him deeply, as his 'wild and whirling words' (I,5) to Horatio indicate, and his decision to feign madness. His despair at having the task of revenge thrust upon him is made vividly clear in his cry of regret that he has been born to carry it out.

Hamlet is also profoundly disturbed by Ophelia's rejection of

his love. In her description of their meetings his feelings for her
seem genuine and deep, not the trifling that Polonius and Laertes fear. Her vivid account of his strange and disturbing
behaviour towards her after her rejection, which reached a
climax in a sigh which 'did seem to shatter all his bulk' (II,1),
reveal the effect upon him of the two shocks he has received so
close one upon the other. Hamlet's disturbed behaviour is
further stressed through the comments of other characters, the
King, the Queen, Polonius, Rosencrantz and Guildenstern. To
them he always seems abnormal. Yet on stage his language and
behaviour alternate between apparent irrationality and perfect
lucidity, giving validity to his own words that the madness is
feigned.

Hamlet appears irrational in his conversations with Polonius,
with Ophelia, and with Rosencrantz and Guildenstern. Yet
beneath the apparent inconsistencies of his words runs a thread
of meaning, a fact which is noticed by Polonius: 'Though this be
madness, yet there is method in't' (II,2). Hamlet's words abound
in sexual references, revealing his obsession with sexual corruption. This is particularly striking in his conversations with
Ophelia, when he likens her to a painted bawd. Through these
conversations the depth of his disgust at his mother's hasty
remarriage is made clear and shown to have had a profound
effect upon his sensibilities. Yet in the midst of irrational
utterances Hamlet can change suddenly into lucid and thoughtful speech, exploring with admiration such subjects as human
reason, and illustrating his thoughts with vivid and beautiful
imagery; this is seen when he describes the air as 'this majestical
roof fretted with golden fire' (II,2), then expresses his disgust at
what human beings have done to it in terms of 'a foul and
pestilent congregation of vapours'. Speeches like this heighten
the presentation of his despair at the world in which he finds
himself.

Hamlet's perception of people is very astute. He realizes
immediately why Rosencrantz and Guildenstern have suddenly
appeared at Court 'You were sent for' (II,2). He trusts them as
he would 'adders fanged' (III,4). In his baiting of Polonius he
shows his awareness of Polonius's meddlesome nature; after he
has accidentally killed him he calls him 'Thou wretched, rash,
intruding fool' (III,4). His understanding of exactly what Osric

is, and his hatred of the vanity and flattery that he embodies, is obvious in the final scene of the play.

Hamlet shows great joy when the Players arrive at Court. His interest in the theatre and his knowledge are clear from his conversation and from his ability to quote, which wins him Polonius's approbation. He also shows a truly warm and sincere affection for the Players themselves, noticing particularly how much the young player, who took the women's parts, has grown and matured. Hamlet's birth never hinders him from enjoying the company of those he likes, regardless of rank. His friendships are based on a recognition of personal qualities, and he never shows superiority about his birth – note his conversation with the Gravediggers. Indeed Claudius recognizes his popularity with the common people. His friendships are strong and true, as is evidenced by the way Horatio supports him throughout the play. He describes in a speech to Horatio that his closest friends will be those whose judgement is balanced, who are not swayed by temper and passion: 'Give me that man, / That is not passion's slave' (III,2).

The Players prompt Hamlet, for the first time in the play, to examine his own inaction and to wonder if he is a coward. He reminds himself again that he must be sure of the origin of the Ghost: 'The Spirit that I have seen may be a devil' (II,2). His self-questioning leads him to devise the plan of using the Players to try to expose the truth about Claudius. How far this is an excuse for his inaction, and how far his hesitation is purely the result of his uncertainty about the Ghost's true identity, has been a subject of debate for many years.

Hamlet's despair at the task assigned to him increases during the play, and in his 'To be' speech, as he again considers suicide, he is clearly world-weary. It is his increasing fearfulness of the unknown, of 'the undiscovered country' that is waiting after death (III,1) that alone causes him to reject suicide. He has become much more fearful than the Hamlet who followed the Ghost at the beginning of the play.

After the King's hasty departure from the Players' performance has convinced Hamlet of Claudius's guilt, he is filled with determination to execute his revenge 'Now could I drink hot blood' (III,2). In his will to be 'cruel not unnatural' he shows his desire for justice and honour, not cold-blooded violence. Never does he descend to the beast-like level of Claudius, who killed for ambition. It is this longing for justice that makes him hesitate when he comes upon Claudius at prayer. For Claudius's sins to be forgiven would destroy the purpose of his death.

It is his mood of determination, and maybe the thought of achieving his aim easily, that leads Hamlet to strike with his sword through the arras in his mother's room. The mistaken killing of Polonius feeds his despair and in a long soliloquy (IV,5) he makes yet another attempt to steel himself for action, encouraged by the reasons he has for the deed and by thoughts of the 'godlike reason' which distinguishes human beings from beasts. Hamlet shows again and again the thoughtful and reflective mind which weighs every reason for action.

In his discussion with his mother Hamlet reveals the depths of his disgust at her behaviour, and a longing that she should realize his feelings. His language towards her becomes so offensive that the Ghost asks him to show restraint. She is convinced that her son is mad, but he rejects this suggestion, insisting that she should end her sexual relationship with Claudius. His words are not those of a madman, but they reveal the intensity of his suffering.

After his return from the journey to England, when he showed courage and determination in escaping from the ship, Hamlet expresses vividly his gift for wit in his conversation with the Gravediggers. Here again, beneath the surface level of the language, he returns through word-play to the theme of human destiny, exploring the idea that after death rank and status have no significance. His words take on a more poignant note as he recalls the jester Yorick, who played with him when he was a child, and he meditates upon the passage of time. This is his last moment of reflection. His realization that the grave being prepared is for Ophelia, and the sight of Laertes's grief, spur him to a wild outburst of activity, and he leaps into the grave to grapple with Laertes.

In the final scene Hamlet faces the duel with Laertes with confidence, and with a sense of acceptance that the outcome will be as destiny wills 'There's a divinity that shapes our ends, / Rough hew them how we will' (V,2). He shows great dignity in his apology to Laertes, and he fights with skill and courage, even when he realizes that the point of Laertes's rapier is poisoned.

He finally avenges his father and kills the King, uttering words that express the extent of his disgust — 'thou incestuous, murderous, damned Dane' (V,2).

Hamlet's death, as he urges Horatio to tell his story, is dignified and moving, and it is fitting that his last words are concerned with the future of Denmark. Horatio's farewell — 'Now cracks a noble heart' — in its simplicity, and Fortinbras's tribute, heighten the tragedy of his death and give it a sense of achievement and finality.

Claudius

And where th'offence is, let the great axe fall (IV,5)

Claudius's first words in the play refer to the death of old Hamlet in a speech whose formality and careful crafting suggest that his grief is not deeply felt. Similarly, the ease with which he dismisses the threat of Fortinbras ('so much for him') and other affairs of state and turns to Laertes, suggests a minimal concern with official duties.

There is even this early in the play a spontaneity and an affection in his words to Laertes that contrast with the reserve of his relationship with Hamlet. He shows little sympathy towards Hamlet's sorrow, urging him not to dwell upon grief as death is natural and goes so far as to hint that Hamlet's mood presents him with a threat. He is anxious that Hamlet should look on him as a father.

The sense of anxiety is reinforced by the length of his speech to Hamlet (I,2), and by his concern to keep Hamlet at Court, under his eye. His refusal to allow Hamlet to return to Wittenburg is striking, coming so soon after his agreement that Laertes should return to his studies in Paris.

His pleasure in feasting and particularly in drinking seems greater than his interest in the state. Hamlet frequently contrasts Claudius with his dead father, citing among his criticisms Claudius's love of drinking which is giving Denmark a bad name abroad (I,4).

Claudius's real nature is made clear to the audience by the Ghost in I,5, in its revelation that it was Claudius who poisoned old Hamlet. This knowledge leads the audience to view Claudius in an unsympathetic manner, and frequently renders his statements ironic.

His devious nature begins to be revealed in his first meeting with Rosencrantz and Guildenstern, as he urges them to spy on Hamlet to try to discover 'if aught to us unknown afflicts him' (II,2). Claudius is clearly anxious to discover the root cause of Hamlet's despair.

His desire to put it right if he can is ironic, and reveals his wish to present himself in a good light. He is continually presented as a man whose interest centres on himself and whose concern for other people is minimal. This is shown again when he dismisses the Ambassadors, saying he will pay attention to their views 'at our more considered time' (II,2). Furthermore, his judgement of people and choice of advisers is shown to be faulty. He considers Polonius to be a man who is 'honourable' (II,1), yet Polonius's plots are far from honourable. Claudius's willingness to comply with Polonius's schemes gives further evidence of his shifty nature and of his anxiety.

Claudius begins to show signs of stress when Ophelia's innocence and Polonius's comment that 'we do sugar o'er the devil himself' (III,1), prompt him to reveal that his conscience is troubling him. By using words like 'harlot', 'ugly', 'painted word' he gives a glimpse of his own self-disgust and creates a moment of sympathy in the audience. This is the first time the audience is given an insight into Claudius's true feelings; his previous appearances on stage have shown only his public face.

The private face is shown again, and more sympathy is generated for him, when he tries to pray. In this speech (III,3) Claudius is shown to be fully aware of the magnitude of his crime, the 'foul murder'; the speech, unlike most of what he says in the play, is fragmented into short sections which make plain the extent of his emotion. This is reinforced by images such as 'this cursed hand', and 'offence's gilded hand', which contrast vividly with his longing for 'rain enough in the sweet heaven to wash it white as snow'. His hope at the end of the speech that 'all will be well' is both pathetic and yet another instance of him turning away from the pressing reality of what he has done.

After this soliloquy the mask descends again. Yet Claudius's continuing anxiety is revealed in his desire to ship Hamlet off to England, where he hopes he will no longer be a threat.

Claudius's response on hearing of Polonius's death 'it had been so with us had we been there' (IV,1) makes plain his awareness of Hamlet's anger and antagonism towards him. From this point in the play he attempts to blacken Hamlet's name, first by emphasizing his madness, and later in the play by making false suggestions to Laertes about Hamlet's behaviour. Here, talking to the Queen, Claudius's image of Hamlet like a 'foul disease' feeding 'even on the pith of life' is violent in its condemnation. This violence finds its outlet in his message to the King of England requesting that Hamlet be put to death. At this point in the play the audience loses all sympathy with Claudius and is fully aware of his hypocrisy, as he suggests to Hamlet that he is to be sent away for 'his especial safety' (IV,3). He shortly afterwards, in the scene with Ophelia, appears little moved by her madness, but again more concerned with its effect upon himself, putting his trust in the divinity that 'doth hedge a king' (IV,5).

He shows himself to be a good diplomat, and by doing so underlines his deceit in his treatment of Laertes later in the play. Claudius allows Laertes to work off his violent energy by letting him speak, flatters him, and finally takes him off to persuade him successfully of his own innocence, thus putting all the blame for Polonius's death and Ophelia's madness on Hamlet.

His self-assurance is momentarily shaken by the letters announcing Hamlet's return, as the broken phrases of his short speeches reveal. He quickly controls himself, however, and divulges to Laertes his plan to kill Hamlet, thus flattering Laertes more by enlisting his help. The extent of his corruption is clear in the dishonourable plot and in his lies, as he attributes to Hamlet an envy of Laertes's skill with a rapier that Hamlet has never expressed.

The evil in his nature is shown dramatically in the final scene when he poisons the wine. He presides over the duel with impassiveness, expressing little emotion, even when the Queen drinks the poisoned wine, attributing her collapse to the sight of blood. His death is quick, allowing the play to concentrate on those characters who show some goodness. There is at the end a sense of justice in Claudius's being killed by Hamlet with the poisoned rapier, a victim of his own plotting and scheming.

The Queen

'O my dear Hamlet . . . I am poisoned' (V,2)

The Queen shows herself at the beginning of the play concerned, and perhaps a little irritated, by Hamlet's refusal to take
part in the marriage celebrations. She is obedient to Claudius's
requests and says little other than to support his suggestions with
her own urgings. Yet she emerges even this early in the play as a
warm and feeling woman, her anxiety about Hamlet deeply felt.

This is shown again in her welcome of Rosencrantz and
Guildenstern and in the way she encourages them to discover
what is affecting her 'too much changed son' (II,2). Her anxiety
is given an ironic touch and greater depth by the audience's
knowledge of old Hamlet's sudden death and her hasty remarriage. Furthermore, her willingness to participate in Claudius's
plan for Rosencrantz and Guildenstern to spy on Hamlet hints
that she may feel partly responsible for his despair. Her anxiety
is revealed again in her slightly irritated request to Polonius to
tell his discoveries with 'more matter' and 'less art' (II,2).

The Queen is genuinely worried about Hamlet's welfare, and
is moved by his appearance as he enters, commenting 'sadly the
poor wretch comes reading' (II,2). She asks anxiously of Rosencrantz and Guildenstern if they have discovered any reason for
his despair. She is warm and gentle with Ophelia, hoping that
she will raise Hamlet's spirits. In contrast to Claudius her
thoughts go out to other people; indeed she serves partly to
underline Claudius's self-centred attitude.

During the Players' performance scene she says very little; her
one comment, 'the lady doth protest too much' (III,2), suggests
that she identifies with the Queen in the play and finds insincere
the Player Queen's insistence that she will never remarry. It is a
hint that the Queen's conscience is troubled.

Prior to the Players' scene the Queen has been on stage a great
deal but she has said very little. She has also been talked about a
great deal by Hamlet; she has been an important element in the
action of the play. Her first independent action is to send for
Hamlet and to agree to Polonius overhearing the conversation.
By allowing Polonius to do this she is shown to be involved in the
corruption of the Court.

Her sympathy towards Hamlet and her patience is by now

growing thinner, revealing how deeply she has been disturbed by the Players' performance. Her changing attitude is shown when she refers to Claudius in her conversation with Hamlet as 'thy father' (III,4); this contrasts vividly with Act I when it was old Hamlet whom she called 'thy noble father'. She is now frightened by Hamlet's behaviour, and her fear and Hamlet's accusations confront her 'like daggers' with such power that for the first time she shows an awareness of the sin that has been committed. Her mention of 'black and grained spots' in her soul expresses vividly her knowledge of what has happened, but she wants to push away that knowledge, repeatedly begging Hamlet to 'speak no more'. Her sensitivity and her love for Hamlet emerge strongly through her emotion and her distress in this scene. In her bewilderment she attributes his behaviour to madness, and it is in these terms that she describes his actions to Claudius. Yet it is noticeable that she hides from Claudius Hamlet's accusations against him.

The Queen's emotion and fear express themselves again when she refuses to see Ophelia, but her natural concern allows her to be easily overruled by Horatio. For a second time she is prompted to reveal her guilt, in an aside. She is strongly affected by Ophelia's state, and in this scene her guilt stands in striking contrast to Ophelia's innocence. This contrast, and the Queen's deeply-felt sorrow for Ophelia, reach a climax in her account of Ophelia's death; the lyricism, the flower and water descriptions, bring out powerfully the Queen's acceptance of her guilt and her involvement. In her expression at the funeral that 'I hoped thou should'st have been my Hamlet's wife' (V,1), she reveals her grief at the innocence that has been lost, and the flowers that she scatters on the grave become symbols of that loss. The tenderness of this element in the play is strengthened by her image of the patient female dove.

Her feelings of guilt and sorrow do not permit her to neglect her duty to Claudius. She gathers together her self-assurance to calm the angry Laertes, and to defend Claudius against any suggestion that he may have been implicated in Polonius's death.

The effect that events have had upon her is shown in the final scene, where for the first time she disobeys Claudius and insists on drinking the wine. In her final words, it is not to Claudius that she turns but to Hamlet, and in saying 'I am poisoned' she acknowledges not only the poisoned wine, but also the sin of her involvement with Claudius. It is a moment of truth, and of tragedy.

Polonius

'Thou wretched, rash, intruding fool' (III,4).

Polonius is a talkative figure, constantly putting forward wisdom which the action of the play shows to be erroneous. He stands as an opposite to Hamlet, his deceit and superficiality contrasting with Hamlet's torment.

His garrulousness is evident from his first words in the play. He employs many adjectives which add little to the meaning of what he is saying; he uses a series of disconnected metaphors and similes and qualifies everything, so that his speeches become laborious and tedious, using many words to convey very little. The Queen draws attention to this when she asks for 'more matter with less art' (II,2). Polonius's verbosity is highlighted by the brevity and simplicity of the language of other characters engaged in dialogue with him.

Polonius has an important position at Court and in the State, and is considered by the King to be 'a man faithful and honourable' (II,2). The confidence placed in him by the King and Queen is evident in their willingness to comply with his suggestions that he should listen in to the conversations between Hamlet and Ophelia and later between Hamlet and the Queen. Yet when Polonius asserts that his opinions have never been proved wrong, the King's response 'not that I know' (II,2) introduces an element of doubt into the audience's perception of his confidence.

Polonius is presented both as a public and as a private figure. His welcome to the Players, full of flattery, is a public welcome, but it contains also a hint of his concern for Hamlet, that the Players may alleviate the 'lunacy' which has afflicted him. His advice to the King and Queen is from his position as Chancellor and friend. He is also shown as a father, caring for the well-being of his children. Yet the true nature of his caring is made suspect.

His advice to Laertes seems sound, but its verbosity

emphasizes Polonius's pompous and complacent nature; this effect is strengthened by the irony of his opening words, urging Laertes to make haste, then delaying him, and by Laertes's unresponsive reply, ignoring his father's words. Polonius's certainty of the value of his advice and judgement is made clear as the scene progresses and he insists to Ophelia that Hamlet is only trifling with her. He gives Ophelia little time to explain her feelings and her point of view, constantly interrupting her and assuring her that he will 'teach' her, in a manner that is both patronizing and insensitive. When he expresses his fear that she will 'tender me a fool' it becomes obvious that self-interest underlies his attitude to both his daughter and son.

His self-interest and conceit lead him to behave in a way that is devious and underhand. Not only is he willing to overhear private conversations, but he goes so far as to urge Reynaldo to spread false gossip about Laertes so that he can discover what his son has been doing in Paris. Reynaldo's shocked response to Polonius's suggestion is emphasized by his position as a servant, and his objection to dishonouring Laertes contrasts strongly with Polonius's complacent attitude. In his long, complex, rambling sentences, Polonius often loses track of his train of thought thus illustrating his lack of concentration and precision. The contrast with Reynaldo's alertness and sense of honour brings out vividly Polonius's weaknesses.

Polonius's conviction in his own judgement receives a jolt when he realizes that he had misjudged Hamlet's love for Ophelia. Yet he uses this to his own advantage and shows his conceit when he tells the King that he has found 'the cause of Hamlet's lunacy' (II,2). His deviousness emerges again, as does his desire to present himself in a good light, when he says that he had told Ophelia that Hamlet's social position made marriage impossible. This is not honourable behaviour.

When the Players appear at Court Polonius tries to show his knowledge and experience of plays. The list of types of plays he gives reveals his desire to seem scholarly, and his comments on the Players' performances show his need to make his presence felt. However by 'tragical-comical-historical-pastoral' (II,2) and by the superficiality of his comments he succeeds only in making himself look ridiculous.

Only Hamlet sees the true nature of Polonius's character. His speeches expose Polonius's lack of honesty, his tediousness, his age and lack of wit, and, in the dialogue about the shape of clouds (III,2), his desire to please and flatter. His death at the hand of Hamlet is ignominious, and the outcome of his deviousness and conceit. It is also fitting, since one of the functions of Polonius in the play is to reflect the self-interest and corruption of the Court, corruption which affects the State and which Hamlet seeks to destroy.

Laertes

'I am justly killed with my own treachery' (V,2).

From his first appearance on the stage Laertes provides a foil for Hamlet. Like Hamlet he is a son, desirous of pursuing his studies abroad. His wish is granted, Hamlet's is not. Like Hamlet he loves Ophelia (though of course as a brother), and like Hamlet he later in the play seeks revenge for the death of his father.

Laertes resembles his father in the lengthy advice he gives to Ophelia, and like Polonius he gives the advice unasked. Like Polonius he means well; his affection for Ophelia is deeply felt. In this conversation with Ophelia his criticism of Hamlet hints at jealousy, expressed strongly through the 'canker' metaphor which ends his speech.

Laertes is absent from the play for much of the action but he reappears towards the end, contrasted again in his behaviour and nature to Hamlet. He is reported to be at the head of a riotous mob of common people, and he bursts onto the stage with a vigour that dramatizes his violent activity. Unlike Hamlet he is a man of action, who never reflects upon life as Hamlet does. He is hot-tempered, and in his anger is abusive to the King, demanding revenge for his father's death with an assurance that has always evaded Hamlet. The hastiness of his temper is illustrated as Claudius easily succeeds in calming him, even after the sight of Ophelia's madness has reinflamed his passion. His flawed judgement of people allows him to be easily convinced by Claudius that Hamlet is not only responsible for Polonius's death, but has also plotted Claudius's death. Unlike Hamlet, Laertes succumbs to Claudius's flattery of him, and in so doing is identified with the corruption that pervades the whole

Danish Court. His quick decisiveness allows him to accept Claudius's proposals for killing Hamlet without hesitation, something which Hamlet would never have been able to do; yet the fact that his decision is the wrong one is clear in the dishonour that results from it, in his decision to go further than Claudius had suggested and fight with a poisoned rapier.

Laertes is capable of deep emotion, as is shown by his reaction to the death of Ophelia. His tears rouse sympathy in the audience, a sympathy which persists as he regrets the absence of ceremony at the burial, and is driven by his grief to leap into her grave.

In the final scene his dignity and courage are sullied by his dishonourable poisoning of the unbated rapier. He represents the corruption of the Court, and is contrasted with Hamlet's courageous and fair fighting. It is this, and the experience of the results of what he has done, that prompt his growing awareness of his treachery, made evident in his comment 'It is almost against my conscience.' This leads him to confess the evil which has been done. He dies, acknowledging his own treachery and revealing the truth, thus heightening the tragedy that Claudius's evil has brought about.

Ophelia

'O woe is me / T'have seen what I have seen, see what I see.' (III,1)

On her first appearance in the play Ophelia is shown as the quiet recipient of the advice of her father and brother who pry into her private life. Yet, while promising to obey them, she shows spirit in telling Laertes not to give advice that he does not intend to follow himself, and in defending Hamlet to her father. Hamlet's strange behaviour terrifies her, but her deep love for him shows through that fear in her sorrow for him; twice she uses the word 'piteous' (II,1) to describe him.

In her conversations with Hamlet (III,1 and 2) Ophelia shows dignity, firmness and simplicity, and a sensitivity which becomes moving as, in a soliloquy, she compares the Hamlet she sees now with the young man that he was. Unlike the King and Queen she does not ask the reasons for his change, but simply grieves deeply over it.

In the Players' scene she exhibits a gentle wit, quietly accepting Hamlet's insults. She is the epitome of goodness. The fact that it is she who first comments on the King's reaction to the Players' performance, saying simply 'The King rises' (III,2) emphasizes the King's guilt in contrast to her own innocence.

The tragedy of the play is heightened by her madness. Her appearance on the stage epitomizes innocence corrupted. Her language, through song and fragmented prose, expresses the death of love; she describes the freshness of flowers and grass, the white purity of snow, then dispels that freshness and purity by mentioning the loss of virginity through deception, and in language that is strongly sexual. This scene forms a stage metaphor for the destruction of goodness.

Her death, vividly described by the Queen in language rich in images of purity and freshness (IV,7) recalls Ophelia's innocence, evoking once more what has been corrupted and destroyed both in the terms of human life, and in a broader sense in the play.

At her funeral her innocence is remembered in the flowers that are scattered on her grave, and is expressed in Laertes's words 'From her fair and unpolluted flesh May violets spring'; his description of her as 'a ministering angel' intensifies the sense of her purity. Yet Ophelia's innocence has not withstood the evil of the world around her, and this is underlined by the omission of funeral rites at her burial, and the Priest's use of the word 'profane' in his refusal of these rites.

Horatio

What is it you would see?
If aught of woe or wonder, cease your search (V,2)

Horatio is a scholar, with considerable knowledge of political events. He arrives from abroad bringing information about what is going on, particularly about Denmark's preparations for war with Norway – which is of course important to the plot. Horatio is important to the structure of the play too in that he listens to Hamlet's account of his escape from the ship to England, and enables this information to be given to the audience.

In the first scene of the play Horatio is presented as a practical man of good sense. He considers that the Ghost is a figment of the Sentinels' imagination. When therefore he is convinced of its reality, the Ghost is given credibility in the play.

Horatio has sensitivity and understanding which make him strongly aware of the implications of the Ghost's appearance. He realizes the threat the Ghost may offer, and presents this vividly in a speech full of words of omen, fear, and descriptions of unusual events, like those that accompanied the murder of Julius Caesar (I,1). His words have the effect of heightening the importance of the Ghost in the play, and of increasing the suspense.

Horatio's concern about the possible implications of the Ghost is made particularly clear when he urges Hamlet not to follow it. His good sense and caution make him fully aware of the dangers Hamlet is courting. He is an old friend of Hamlet's and in his worry that the Ghost might 'deprive your sovereignty of reason, And draw you into madness' (I,5) he reveals an awareness of Hamlet's nature and a warm, caring affection for him. By the use of these words Horatio also shows an uncanny insight into future events in the play.

Horatio is Hamlet's frequent companion and the only person whom he trusts. He it is whom Hamlet asks to watch Claudius in the Players' scene, he it is to whom Hamlet sends letters announcing his return from England. He accompanies Hamlet through the two final scenes of the play, supporting him and listening to him. His concern shows itself again in his fear that Hamlet is no match for Laertes in the duel, and this again has the effect of heightening the suspense of that scene.

At the end of the play Horatio shows his deep love for Hamlet by wanting to end his life with Hamlet's by drinking the poisoned wine. By this wish he shows a courage that underlines Hamlet's earlier vacillation in the play; Hamlet was unable to steel himself to commit suicide. His love is emphasized again as he agrees to Hamlet's dying words that Horatio should not die, but live on to 'tell my story' (V,2). As in the first scene Horatio talked of the 'fear and wonder' that the Ghost aroused in him, so at the end he talks of Hamlet in terms of 'woe and wonder'. His words in their praise of Hamlet heighten the tragedy of his death; his straightforward simplicity and honesty makes his phrase 'Now cracks a noble heart' a fitting epitaph.

It is the continuation of the qualities that he represents which suggests, at the end of the play, a move forward into a better world.

Rosencrantz and Guildenstern

'You cannot play upon me' Hamlet (III,2)

Rosencrantz and Guildenstern are indistinguishable from one another, and attention is drawn to this by the Queen's repetition of the King's thanks to them, only substituting the names (II,2). The impossibility of distinguishing them gives them a mediocrity almost from their first appearance in the play.

Like Horatio they are old friends of Hamlet, and they are greeted warmly by Hamlet on his first meeting with them. They are, however, totally different from Horatio in character. They are aligned with Claudius from their arrival at Court, and presented in corrupt terms straightaway as they agree to find out for Claudius what afflicts Hamlet.

While Horatio is a trusted friend, Hamlet is quickly suspicious of Rosencrantz and Guildenstern; he easily extracts from them the reason they have been invited to Court; in contrast, they are unable to discover what it is that affects Hamlet so deeply.

As the play proceeds Hamlet treats them with increasing contempt. In Act III Scene 2 he draws attention to their inadequacies, asking 'Have you any further trade with us?'. The word 'trade' has associations in the play with prostitution, and thus Hamlet is linking their business with him with the corruption in the play, and underlining the disgust he feels at their activities. Through the metaphor of the recorder Hamlet emphasizes that they are unable to manipulate him: 'You cannot play upon me.'

By Act IV Hamlet has them completely at his mercy; 'I understand you not' says Rosencrantz, stressing how much Hamlet is superior to them. Their executions organized by Hamlet, are just, and contribute towards Hamlet's revenge.

Osric

Dost thou know this waterfly? (V,2)

Osric is a courtier, dressed extravagantly, and he symbolizes the nature of Claudius's Court. His language is verbose, repetitive and full of unimaginative words of excess like 'very' and 'great', 'absolute' and 'most'. He is too vain, too full of himself and too foolish to realize how Hamlet baits him, and in his desire to flatter and please, contradicts himself, underlining his insincerity and lack of truth. He represents wordliness, mediocrity and hypocrisy, those qualities to which Hamlet is most strongly opposed, and he underlines the contrast between Hamlet, and those people with whom Claudius has surrounded himself.

His additional function is to provide humour, to lighten the tension as the play approaches its climax, and, by making a pause in the action, to add to the sense of suspense.

Style and structure

Structure

The play is constructed by means of contrasts. The opening scene is one of darkness and quiet, with few characters on stage. This scene is followed by something quite different, a public, crowded stage, with all the royalty and nobility of the Court present, set off by their rich, elaborate clothes and the splendour of the court setting. Throughout the play scenes form contrasts with one another, giving external, public views which alternate with intimate, personal glimpses. Scenes of action, such as Hamlet's following of the Ghost, the Players' scenes, the arrival of Laertes at Court, the final duel scene, and the coming and going of characters, are contrasted with scenes of inaction, such as the conversations of Hamlet with the King and Queen, with Ophelia, with the Gravediggers, his many soliloquies, and Polonius's conversations with Laertes and Ophelia.

Contrast is also the means used to present the central figure, Hamlet, and to throw his character into relief. Hamlet's inaction, and his reflective, thoughtful nature, are emphasized by the contrasting active, quick-tempered spontaneity of Laertes. Both are put into the position of having to avenge their fathers' deaths. Hamlet spends most of the play summoning up the will to carry out his revenge, while Laertes arrives noisily and angrily at Court, determined to commit the act of revenge immediately, with no pause for thought. Fortinbras too, another man of action, with his skill in battle, shows up Hamlet's inability to carry out even one act of personal revenge.

Hamlet's inaction is contrasted also with the decisiveness of Claudius, who puts one plan after another into operation in his efforts to fulfil his ambition and secure his position. These two characters are opposite too in their attitudes to justice: Hamlet is obsessed with justice and with acting rightly (shown in his need to discover if the Ghost's words are true), while Claudius is ever willing to carry out acts of corruption to attain his own ends. Hamlet's search during the early part of the play is for the truth about his father's death, Claudius's search meanwhile is to discover how much Hamlet knows.

Claudius is also contrasted with old Hamlet. In the early scenes remarks made by Horatio, Barnardo and Marcellus illustrate the differences between the two Kings: Hamlet is, in Horatio's words, 'a goodly king' (I,2), whilst Claudius prefers revelry (I,4). The contrast between the two is made particularly clear in the scene with Hamlet and his mother; when he produces portraits of them both he brings out Hamlet's perfection in a comparison with the great classical gods, and Claudius's inadequacies and weaknesses, 'like a mildew'd ear,/Blasting his wholesome brother' (III,4).

The madness which affects two characters induces a deeper understanding of the meaning of the play. Ophelia's madness is real, caused by the change in Hamlet and the death of her father. Hamlet's madness is feigned, rational and controlled. This contrast serves to underline the tragedy of Ophelia, of her lost happiness and innocence, and extends these dual losses into the whole play, so that they become associated with the humankind's conflict between innocence and corruption. This is further shown in the conflict between madness and lucidity in Hamlet's own speech.

One of the themes of the play is death. The structure of the play emphasizes this by dramatizing death on the stage. The coming of the Ghost, in the darkness of the night on the battlements, demonstrates Hamlet's thoughts about death, his fear of the unknown, the threat of death. Later in the play when Hamlet's experiences have made him less afraid of death, the graveyard scene creates a different mood. The daylight and the cheerful talk of the Gravediggers, their jokes, their total acceptance of death as an everyday occurrence, the handling of the skulls by both them and Hamlet, Hamlet's warm, happy memories of Yorick, all contribute towards an acceptance of death.

Imagery

The prolific imagery of the play brings out the contrasting themes of goodness and corruption, of reason and instinct, and the subject of violence, and enables communication at a deep and subtle level.

The existence of goodness, of a sense of justice and right, of innocence and beauty, is suggested through a variety of images. Beauty is seen in the warm colour of Horatio's metaphor for the dawn 'in russet mantle clad' (I,1), in the richness and musical harmony of the 'golden couplets' of the 'patient' 'female dove' by which Gertrude describes Hamlet (V,1), in the colour of the sky 'fretted with golden fire' (II,2) in Hamlet's description of the world as it ought to be. The light of the stars in this same speech suggests beauty, constancy and order, and also human reason which can pierce through the darkness of corruption and evil. This sense is present too in the dawn metaphor, and in the light of the glow worm which illuminates the darkness of the night (I,5). It is extended further by the simile of the gods Jove, Mars and Mercury, to whom the dead Hamlet is likened (III,4). He is endowed with a greatness which is above the pettiness of human corruption represented by Claudius.

The theme of innocence and purity in the play is illustrated by the imagery of flowers which is associated with Ophelia, those that she gives to the people at Court, those that surround her at her death, and those that are scattered on her grave. Water, with its purifying quality, enriches her death, both the water of the brook and the water of her tears. Associated with Ophelia too is music, in the songs that she sings in her mad scenes and as she drowns; music brings a sense of harmony into these scenes of the play.

These images of beauty, order, innocence, purity and harmony are, however, overwhelmed by contrasting images of corruption, as the 'sweet bells' by which Ophelia describes Hamlet's 'noble and most sovereign reason' are 'jangled out of tune and harsh' (III,1).

The dominating images in the play are of disease and dirt. Hamlet refers to his mother's sin as an 'ulcerous place' which 'infects' all around it, and as a 'blister' (III,4). The war between Denmark and Norway is described as a 'tumour'; 'sickly day', 'foul disease', 'plurisy' are used to describe Claudius, and the state and its people are referred to as a 'sick body'. The beauty of the sky has become to Hamlet nothing but 'a foul and pestilent congregation of vapours' (II,2). Disease in plants is used too: Laertes refers to the love of Hamlet for Ophelia as 'a canker' (I,3); weeds which have grown to excess and are 'rank' are mentioned on several occasions.

Dirt is associated with disease imagery to extend the sense of corruption. The people under Claudius's rule are described as 'muddied', and Hamlet refers to his own inaction in terms of being 'muddy-mettled'. The Queen recognizes her guilt in terms of 'black and grained spots' (III,4).

Her actions are described by Hamlet using imagery of prostitution, and he imposes upon Ophelia his horror at his mother's behaviour using the same imagery of sexual corruption, referring to her in terms of 'bawd', and 'paintings' (III,2). This pattern is extended by imagery linked with trade, used particularly by Polonius in his conversation with Ophelia (I,2); he picks up the word 'tender' and uses it to suggest that Ophelia is allowing her virtue to be demeaned: 'You have ta'en these tenders for true pay/That are not sterling.'

Hamlet takes up again the imagery of corruption in a horrifying manner, referring to Ophelia in terms of 'breeding maggots in a dead dog'. This incorporates the sexual theme with corruption and death and underlines animal instincts. There are several other angel/beast references in the play and these highlight Hamlet's concern for godlike human reason as opposed to animal instincts.

The Queen's excess of sexual appetite and its disastrous import is emphasized through imagery of feeding. The Ghost talks of lust which will 'prey on garbage' (I,5). Claudius makes clear his fear of Hamlet by describing his 'foul disease' which 'feeds on the pith of life'. The Ghost describes vividly his death by poisoning in terms of milk, with its associations of the innocence and helplessness of a baby, being polluted and curdled (I,5).

Imagery of war helps create an atmosphere of violence in the play. Hamlet develops a metaphor of warfare in his 'To be' soliloquy (III,1). He talks of the onslaught of fortune in terms of 'slings and arrows' and of 'taking arms' against trouble; of changing the Queen's behaviour, unless it be 'proof and bulwark' against his words (III,4). He speaks of the 'pales and forts of reason' (I,4) when he describes a particular flaw in human beings that can override their judgement.

The imagery in the play is rich and complex, and suggests threads and depths which enable the language to function at different levels.

The soliloquy

Among Shakespeare's plays *Hamlet* is particularly rich in soliloquies, spoken mostly by Hamlet himself. Claudius's words of prayer have the effect of a soliloquy, and Ophelia has one soliloquy when she describes Hamlet as he used to be, and expresses her grief at the change in him.

The soliloquy serves the dramatic purpose of creating a moment of quiet in the play. There is a sense of intimacy and privacy when one character is speaking alone on the stage. It is an opportunity for a character to reveal to the audience his or her real feelings, and also an opportunity for information to be given. This can have an important dramatic effect: when the Players perform Hamlet's play the audience is already aware from Claudius's attempt to pray, that he is guilty of the murder of old Hamlet, and is encouraged to watch carefully the reactions of both him and Hamlet during the scene.

Ophelia, in her soliloquy (III,1), underlines the change in Hamlet, which emphasizes the stress which he is suffering and increases the audience's sympathy for him. She also reveals the depth of her love for Hamlet, heightening the tragedy and adding poignancy to the play. By being alone on the stage, with attention fastening upon her, her role in the play, her innocence and purity, are given a central focus.

It is Hamlet's soliloquies that are of particular importance. They concentrate the audience's attention upon him and highlight his position as the central character in the play. His tormented thoughts and feelings are revealed in all their intimacy, and create a sensitivity and sympathy for him in his struggle to commit an act for which he feels himself totally unfitted. They also reveal the strength of his hatred for Claudius, his utter disgust at his mother's sexual relationship with Claudius, and his admiration for his dead father.

They make plain his fear of death, his horror of the unknown which death presents, and they enable the audience to be aware of his thoughtful considerations of the nature of death, and of the nature of human life. It is in his soliloquies that Hamlet reflects upon the quality of human reason and how reason differentiates the human being from the beast.

The use of verse and prose

The majority of *Hamlet* is written in blank verse, poetry written in the form of iambic pentameters, with five stressed syllables in each line, and usually without rhyme. There are however sometimes, particularly at the end of a scene, pairs of rhyming couplets, which give a feeling of culmination to a speech. Shakespeare's blank verse is fluent and has a natural rhythm, but its form imposes upon it a heightened quality; this is intensified by the use of imagery and other poetic forms in the language. Characters of noble birth almost always speak in blank verse.

Characters of lower birth, like the Players and the Grave-diggers, show their status by speaking not in blank verse but in prose. This provides a contrast in the play which adds variety, and also contributes a simplicity and a warmth to these figures. Hamlet speaks in prose with these characters too, indicating his natural ease in communicating with ordinary working people.

Prose also gives Shakespeare an opportunity to introduce humour into the play. The wit, the misuse of language, the straightforward merriment of the Gravediggers, are rendered more vivid and appealing by the varying lengths of phrase and the broken lines and rhythms of the prose.

Humour of a different sort is indicated when characters of a higher rank speak in prose. Osric's pretentiousness and petti-ness are emphasized by the prose of his speech. In contrast, when he announces the arrival of Fortinbras, an event of great significance in the play, he speaks in blank verse (V,2). Polonius and Rosencrantz and Guildenstern are ridiculed when they use prose in their scenes with Hamlet when he is feigning madness. They speak in prose to humour Hamlet but succeed in appearing patronizing, and are played with and made to look foolish by him.

Prose is the language of madness and is used by Ophelia in her mad scenes to indicate that her reason has been shattered, that she has lost all control over her faculties. Her use of prose makes her situation all the more moving and pathetic.

Madness is associated in the play with disorder. The prose which follows Hamlet's meeting with the Ghost (I,5) underlines the sense of disorder which is dramatized by the appearance of the Ghost. At this point the prose also adds to the mood of fear, uncertainty and excitement.

During his conversation with Rosencrantz and Guildenstern Hamlet's prose (II,2) illustrates his uncertainty and despair as he describes 'this goodly frame, the earth' being nothing more than 'a sterile promontory' and man with his faculties and reason being nothing more than 'this quintessence of dust'. The evil committed by Claudius is affecting the whole universe.

Further reading

The Arden Shakespeare: Hamlet, ed. H. Jenkins (Methuen, 1982)

Shakespearean Tragedy, A. C. Bradley (Macmillan, 1905)

Shakespeare, A. Burgess (Penguin, 1972)

The Development of Shakespeare's Imagery, W. Clemen (University Paperbacks, 1951)

Shakespeare's Imagery, C. Spurgeon (Cambridge University Press, 1935)

What Happens in Hamlet, J. D. Wilson (Cambridge University Press, 1951)

Principles of Shakespearean Production, G. Wilson Knight (Penguin, 1936)

Notes

Notes

Notes

Notes

Pan study aids Titles published in the Brodie's Notes series

E. Albee Who's Afraid of Virginia Woolf?

Jane Austen Emma Pride and Prejudice

Robert Bolt A Man for All Seasons

Harold Brighouse Hobson's Choice

Charlotte Brontë Jane Eyre Villette

Emily Brontë Wuthering Heights

Geoffrey Chaucer (parallel texts editions) The Nun's Priest's Tale
The Pardoner's Tale Prologue to the Canterbury Tales
The Wife of Bath's Tale

Bruce Chatwin On the Black Hill

Gerald Cole Gregory's Girl

Charles Dickens David Copperfield Great Expectations Oliver Twist

George Eliot Silas Marner

T. S. Eliot Murder in the Cathedral

F. Scott Fitzgerald The Great Gatsby

E. M. Forster A Passage to India

John Fowles The French Lieutenant's Woman

William Golding Lord of the Flies

Graham Green Brighton Rock

Thomas Hardy Far from the Madding Crowd
The Mayor of Casterbridge Tess of the d'Urbervilles

Susan Hill I'm the King of the Castle

Barry Hines Kes

James Joyce A Portrait of the Artist as a Young Man

John Keats Selected Poems and Letters of John Keats

D. H. Lawrence Sons and Lovers

Harper Lee To Kill a Mockingbird

Laurie Lee Cider with Rosie

Christopher Marlowe Doctor Faustus

Arthur Miller The Crucible Death of a Salesman

Bill Naughton Spring and Port Wine

Robert C. O'Brien Z for Zachariah

George Orwell Animal Farm 1984

J. B. Priestley An Inspector Calls

J. D. Salinger The Catcher in the Rye

William Shakespeare Antony and Cleopatra As You Like It
Coriolanus Hamlet Julius Caesar King Lear Macbeth
The Merchant of Venice A Midsummer Night's Dream Othello
Romeo and Juliet The Tempest Twelfth Night

G. B. Shaw Pygmalion

John Steinbeck Of Mice and Men & The Pearl

Keith Waterhouse Billy Liar

John Webster The White Devil

Tennesee Williams A Streetcar Named Desire

GCSE English Coursework: Prose G. Handley and P. Wilkins

GCSE English Coursework: Drama and Poetry K. Dowling